Inching To Wisdom

Mostly True Stories

by

J. Eva Nagel

To my Grandma Charlotte whose love made all the
difference
To those who have inspired, guided and cared for
me
To the next generations, with apologies and hope
To the blessings of beauty that are all around me
To the spirit of hope and the hope of healing
I am grateful for this journey

Janet,

May you keep on inching forward Towards wisdom, joy & laughter!

Eva B

All food photographs are courtesy of Nirinjan Kaur Khalsa, the oldest, and possibly the wisest, of the cousins, (who hold their own cousin's summit whenever they get together). I am so grateful that she brought her considerable talent to bear on illuminating the recipes here. The pictures are beautiful and, I promise you, the food will be almost as delicious as it looks.

Cover design by Shanti R. Nagel with formatting by Avi B. Nagel.

Book content formatted and edited and edited again by Kiara Nagel.

Table of Contents

had become a raging river. Just as we breathed a sigh of relief, a half dozen tools and one large windshield tumbled out of the wide-open back to crash upon the aforementioned ice.

Of the six windshields in Ralph's van, wouldn't you know it, the one that shattered was ours, leaving me without a windshield or a car. It could have been worse. No falls, no lawsuits, and no vans sailing downriver was a good thing, and thanks to the wonders of modern laminated windshields, no shards of glass spewed across our driveway. We counted our frosty blessings and got on the waiting list for the next available windshield.

You see, this proves my point—most of us really are inching towards wisdom, although some days it seems we slide in the utterly wrong direction.

What follows is a loosely connected collection of essays about my life thus far. You will find babies, trauma, travel, and maybe even a few glimmers of actual wisdom. And sprinkled in here and there are some family recipes because, after all, even the wisest of us must stop and eat. Please enjoy, and don't forget to keep counting your own hard won wisdom.

> *The miracle is not to walk on water.*
> *The miracle is to walk on the green earth,*
> *dwelling deeply in the present moment and*
> *feeling truly alive.*
>   Thich Nhat Hanh

Today I had arranged for our old Honda's windshield to be replaced. A small ding had grown into a long, creeping crack. Do you know that those windshield guys come right to your house now? The technician, let's just call him Ralph, called at 8 AM to tell me he would call me back with his ETA. At 9:30 I called him because my niece needed the car later to get to work. He had one more job and would be coming after that, he assured me. One hour later, he called to ask how to put my address into his GPS. It doesn't always work out here, I told him. He proceeded to fall apart—if it wasn't in his GPS, he couldn't find it, he complained. I attempted to give him directions—it really was quite simple—and he kept suggesting a different way to put it in his GPS. Damn if this didn't prove my husband's theory that smartphones make people stupid. Fast-forward another forty-five minutes and he arrived, distracted and annoyed and got to work.

Following a week of sub-arctic weather, it was pouring rain, and our long, curving driveway had turned into a translucent river of ice. After removing the cracked windshield from our little Honda, parked cozily in the garage, Ralph went back to root around in his van. Just as he stepped away, the van slid, not so slowly, down the driveway. We both held our breath as the van glided to a halt inches from our ditch, which

INTRODUCTION: TWO STEPS FORWARD AND A BIG SLIDE BACK

It is the middle of January, bitter cold, and I have been trying to figure out how to introduce myself. Do I tell you the story of my life? No, I've lived too long. Do I say that I was born in Oklahoma (yippee yi-aye!) but grew up in Upstate New York (brrr)? Do I slip into the conversation that I finished high school in three years so I could get the hell out of my provincial hometown? Or that I came back to settle into an old farmhouse in that self-same town and have not budged in more than thirty years? Talk about provincial. Do I describe children, now grown, or grandkids still growing? Do I list the pros and cons of aging or spare you those tired adages? I could discuss Waldorf Education or the Trauma Resource Institute. Do I tell you about my fledgling art projects and hope you are sensitive to the fact that I am easily discouraged by sightings of real talent? Perhaps I should offer some wise advice: eat breakfast, cut down on sugar, don't forget to laugh a lot, except at your partner when he is trying to tell you something serious. Instead, I just want to tell you what happened today, about the small moments that creep, scrabble, and fumble towards wisdom.

ROOTS

Shorty

One dark January morning, my world tipped — really it was more like a yawning chasm opened and I fell in. I awoke to find my 3 1/2-year-old sister dead. Funny how quickly one's world changes with no rumble of distant thunder or ominous news of mobilizing armies. I went to bed. She was fine. The next morning, I woke up to a disappeared sister. And nothing, pretty much nothing, would ever be the same.

Her name was Laura, but I called her Shorty. Even at three years old, she filled the room. Her commands organized our frantic mornings as her four older siblings scrambled to leave for school. She ordered Peter to finish his milk and Steven to take his notebook from the counter. Watching my mother knit, she demanded yarn and needles and could not be deterred by suggestions that she needed to wait until she was older. "Mommy, I really can't wait," she answered. Dressed up in my awkward best as I prepared for a school dance, she once gazed at me and sighed, "You are so bloo-ful-oo!" At that time, she was the only one who thought so.

At thirteen, I was a tentative adolescent, awkward and cautious. It was the early '60's when my innocence was, for just a little longer, possible. Charlie Brown and Dick Van Dyke were on TV, and our own personal Top 40 Countdown was broadcast from the family room every Friday night by my big brother Steven, complete with commentary and breathless anticipation. I wasn't allowed to stay up, so I listened from my bedroom. It was really the top 12 or 13, hampered by the limits of our pooled allowance for buying 45's. The Everly Brothers crooned, "Wake up little Suzy." And Lesley Gore sang, "It's my party and I'll cry if I want to." As I began to emerge from my pre-teen, gawky stage, I didn't always want to be home with my baby sister. Her imperious call, issued from beneath raised arms, no longer brought me running. It was other hands I dreamed of holding. Trudging home after school to her flying leap of greeting was not quite as satisfying as it once was. I was looking past her into the wider world.

Sometimes I believe that I ordered Laura. She was the smartest, cutest sister available. When I was six, my mother called me from the hospital to tell me her good news: I had a new baby brother. "That's no fair!" I whined. "I already have two brothers." I wanted a sister. Six years later, my wish came true. And I loved her completely.

But that night in January, I had a dream and awakened early in the morning to see my parents crushed into the corner, Dad disappearing behind Mom in her hideous green mu–mu. I am not sure if I always despised the mu-mu or if it was only after that fateful morning. I sat up. "Laura's dead," I yelped. Maybe I heard something in the night; maybe I dreamed it. My mother's knees buckled, and her coughing filled the room. They bustled me off to see Dr. Mintzer, our neighbor and pediatrician, who had been called in the night, but failed to keep my sister alive. He prescribed me pills. The previous summer my dog Queenie was hit by a car, and he gave me those pills. I had slept a dark molasses sleep, waking every hour to discover all over again that Queenie was dead. I wanted nothing to do with that form of oblivion. This time around, I refused medication.

Death illuminates a flattened world. In the days after my sister's death, I had to navigate the new landscape. I slept at home but lived with Debbie Poukish in the yellow house on the next street. There was air to breathe over there, and her parents talked in normal voices. I went to school, walked down the halls, sang in the choir, did occasional homework, and chuckled to myself about how easy it was to fool everyone. They thought it was the real me, that I was actually there and OKAY. But I was off somewhere else looking for a place where life made sense, where evil was punished, and good rode off into the sunset.

No one wanted to talk to me anyway. Teachers looked away, friends joked more loudly, neighbors pasted on frozen smiles of concern. Most of the time, I pretended I was invisible. I longed to curl up in my grandmother's lap, but my legs were too long and my rear end too bony. It wasn't me she wanted to hold anyway.

There was a funeral service. The words droned on, but the language was indecipherable. When the pallbearers picked up her tiny coffin, it tipped, and I laughed. And the laugh grew louder and louder until Phyllis, our sort-of second mother, escorted me quickly out. Who were they fooling? My little sister was not in that sharp-edged box. That box should be used to ship office supplies or newly hatched baby chicks. Why hadn't they punched air holes in the top? After that, they didn't allow me to go to the cemetery. They said it would upset me, but I was fine as I watched from behind my bulletproof shield. My laughter had unhinged something in the room, but not in me.

A cause of death was never determined. She was alive with a slight cold, and then, in the middle of the night, she was dead like a branch snapped in winter's ice. My mother, a nurse, performed CPR until the EMT guys pulled her away. The resulting cough would stay with her for the rest of her long life.

My parents—modern, law-abiding liberals—had no use for God or any of the trappings of religion. They believed in: *Do unto others as you would have them do unto you* and *Help those who are less fortunate.* It worked well until my sister disappeared. What do you say to random tragedy? Our family flew apart as fast as an exploding meteorite. Dad went into his isolated office world. Mom descended into an almost madness that went from let's-pretend-life-as-usual to a silent, unwashed lockdown so quickly I got whiplash. She placed an invisible, flashing neon sign in our house that read, "Do not speak Laura's name." Steven went to a friend's house, and Jay and Peter into the basement. I couldn't bear to be home—the echoes of silence were deafening. If I got too near to my big brother, I risked electrocution from cold sparks of anger, and the bewilderment of my two younger brothers could not become my problem. I had to save myself, and I was sinking fast.

I searched for people on the periphery. Mrs. Trombley, my piano teacher, was one. I wanted her matter-of–fact Methodist faith. She talked to me. We lived around the corner from a seminary. One day, I had a conversation with a young, visiting priest. "God must have wanted her for his very own," he told me kindly. *Yes!* I wanted to imagine heavenly peace and Laura up there laughing with God, but what kind of a selfish God is that?? I needed her for myself. He could have at least waited. This led to an especially vivid picture of God and me playing tug of war with my

5

tousled sister—my hands encircling her waist, God holding on to one dimpled baby-fist as my grasp inexorably slips and she is dragged away. "But I want her," I would pathetically cry as she and God faded away to heaven leaving me and my pimples still very much on earth.

There were long nights in that pink bedroom that now appeared to belong to someone else—someone childish and frivolous. Long nights spent in angry debates with God—*OKAY, if you are there, speak up now. Why would you do this? Give me a sign, something to believe.* I cried in that room; everyplace else was off limits. Body spread-eagle, I lay there staring at the ceiling imagining my own death with people weeping over me and praising my goodness. It should have been me. Did God screw up? He took the prettier, smarter sister, the one everyone loved. The grim reaper probably came for me in the night and left with Laura by mistake.

Though the nights were endless, at least they were mine. Through the wall, I could hear Mom snoring in a drugged stupor. Dad, with relentless insomnia, was downstairs pacing from kitchen to den and back again. Big brother, angry and dangerous, came sneaking in through the basement window after his late-night prowls. And pathetic me, sailing through on a sea of traitorous pink, was trying to remember a little sister I once had and the life she had stolen from me.

I would have to be good forever. Or maybe it no longer mattered how I behaved. This is what happens when there is no ground to stand on, like when you wake up in your own bedroom knowing exactly where you are, having traversed this landscape for years, and you reach out for the wall to find nothing. Your hand

6

stretches into the void flailing for something solid. It is as if you have stepped off the world into a map-less land where even the shadow of your once-familiar hand in front of your own face can no longer be distinguished. All is darkness. "And the earth was without form, and void; and darkness was upon the face of the deep." (Genesis)

I think I began my life's search for God, for meaning, for spirit, right then. I knew there had to be something more. I made a vow that I would never shy away from or avoid talking about death. I refused to join the silent zombie trail of tears. I would be there for others, and I would talk about my sister with joy and laughter.

At last, spring arrived, and three things happened that made all the difference.

1. I got contact lenses.
2. Jimmy Clark appeared... my very own boyfriend!
3. The Beatles. Oh yes, The Beatles.

O please, say to me, you'll let me hold your hand.
Now, let me hold your hand, I want to hold your hand.

Blasting out of the jukebox at PJ's, those lyrics pulsed in my icy veins and kept me alive. I was like a Tickle-Me-Elmo doll needing to be squeezed or shaken to feel anything. My sister was cold in her grave, and I wanted to be out having fun. I began to live a double life: brooding and mournful at home, increasingly wild everywhere else. I cultivated the divine art of deception. What was wrong with me? I tried to stop. Every night, I promised God that I would be serious and repent. But flirting was a wonder drug, and I was powerless to resist. Was this the devil? Would I burn in hell? Maybe Shorty gave her life for me. Maybe she was my Jesus, my Abraham. Or was she a siren luring me to the pleasures of the flesh—well not much flesh yet, but a breathtaking glimpse of possibility?

April arrived with daffodils and my birthday. What a surprise. Fourteen. Life had not stopped. Later that week, three months after I awoke to a sister-less world and a family that would never be able to heal, I broke into my own house. My parents were away for the day, and there was something I had to do. Jimmy was my accomplice. I was terrified of getting caught. My mother was not someone you wanted to cross. The clear, unspoken commandment in our house was— *Thou shall not make mention of a certain dead child.* Her name was never spoken aloud. Getting into my empty house was easy. I made a beeline for the hall closet. Working like a well-oiled machine, we pulled the shades and prepared. No, not what you might expect from two newly in love teenagers. We were not there for any hanky panky but to set up the projector. Finally I sat, tears rolling down my cheeks, laughter flying skyward, as I watched my sister running across the portable screen—alive and beautiful in our home movies. Now I knew for sure: there was no way that she was in that horrid box.

Father Sang the World to Me

My father was a man of few words. He was shy, thoughtful, and often silent. He could get through an entire meal at the family table overflowing with five kids, one wife, and a dog (underneath) without uttering more than a *yes, no,* or *please pass the ketchup.* After dinner, he quickly disappeared into the den where he sat with one neatly pressed leg crossed over the other and the latest library book on his lap. Out in the world, he was a professional esteemed for his honesty and righteousness, but in my years as a young girl, I mostly heard his silence.

I can picture him clearly—regal sweep of Kennedy-style hair, tailored clothes, and a wiry, fit body. Though we did not talk much, every few weeks my father came unexpectedly alive. I waited and watched for those times. The nearly inaudible notes emerging from our stereo player alerted me.

It's show time, I'd whisper to myself. Dropping whatever I was doing and abandoning whomever I was doing it with; I'd slip ghost-like into the living room. There I'd sit in silence, partially hidden by the piano, with an unobstructed view of my father. The record was already in place, and after carefully closing the curtains, my father would face the stereo as if it was his co-star and begin to sing.

> *Maybe the sun gave me the power*
> *For I could swim Loch Lomond*
> *and be home in half an hour*
> *Maybe the air gave me the drive*
> *For I'm all aglow and alive*

9

That is such a sweet love song from *Brigadoon.*
At first, I could barely hear him, so hushed was his
singing that it was almost a whisper. But before long,
his baritone was in full employ, overflowing the room.
That's when the gestures began. By that time, he had
an abandon I never saw anyplace else. And once he was
singing, I could step out and sing alongside him.
Nothing could stop him now.

What a day this has been,
What a rare mood I'm in
Why, it's almost like being in love
There's a smile on my face
For the whole human race
Why, it's almost like being in love
All the music of life seems to be
like a bell that is ringing for me.

And from the way that I feel
When that bell starts to peal
I could swear I was falling,
I would swear I was falling
It's almost like being in love

I had no idea at the time that it was happening,
but my father taught me about life during these sing-a-
longs. He never sat me down to give me a forced lesson
of imparted wisdom nor did he demand that I pay
attention. But he did manage to pass on his beliefs.
Some fathers teach their children with a bible, others
use the whip, and there are those that give long, boring
lectures. My father sang the world to me. It was a world
of struggle and challenges, sorrows and longings, but it
was a world where happy endings were not only
possible, they were required. His singing filled me with

10

the certainty that I could do anything, be anything. His songs showed me that amidst the sorrow and injustices that I felt too deeply, there existed the possibility of redemption.

Let me give you an example. He rarely told me that he loved me or covered me in wet kisses. He was not that kind of man. But he sang to me, with me, and for me! Like this one from *Guys and Dolls*:

> *I love you a bushel and a peck*
> *A bushel and a peck*
> *And a hug around the neck*
> *A hug around the neck*
> *And a barrel and a heap*
> *A barrel and a heap*
> *And I'm talkin' in my sleep*
> *About you, about you*
> *'Cause I love you a bushel and a peck*
> *You bet your purdy neck I do*
> *A doodle oodle ooh doo*
> *A doodle oodle oodle ooh doo*

Though at some point when I grew older, I knew about his work with our local NAACP and heard about his legendary honesty, he didn't often declare to me his deep convictions about justice and freedom. Yet from him and his singing, I learned:

> *You've got to be taught to hate and fear*
> *You've got to be taught from year to year*
> *It's got to be drummed*
> *In your dear little ear.*
>
> *You've got to be carefully taught*

You've got to be taught to be afraid
Of people whose eyes are oddly mad,
And people whose skin
Is a diff'rent shade

You've got to be carefully taught.
You've got to be taught before it's too late
Before you are six or seven or eight
To hate all the people your relatives hate
You've got to be carefully taught

Can you believe that Rodgers and Hammerstein wrote that for *South Pacific* in 1949, right after the war? It is still right on the mark.

I think I set out then and there to change the world. I was just a young girl, so what did I know of loss and suffering? I didn't even know about my father's sorrows. His time in the army during World War II was never mentioned. He did not speak about the daughter who died or the mother he never saw. But I knew that hate, racism, and injustice were wrong and that the world needed people willing to stand up for what was right.

This was important and intriguing, but it was nothing compared to the joy and excitement that spread through the vibrating floorboards as we came in for the grand finale. Boy, did I love the happy endings! My dad and I— we could belt it out almost as loud as Ethel Merman in *Gypsy*.

You'll be swell, you'll be great
Gonna have the whole world on a plate
Starting here, starting now
Honey everything's coming up roses

Clear the decks, clear the tracks
You've got nothing to do but relax
Blow a kiss, take a bow
Honey everything's coming up roses

Now's your inning,
Stand the world on its ear
Set it spinning,
That'll be just the beginning
Curtain up, light the lights
You got nothing to hit but the heights

You can do it, all you need is a hand
We can do it, mama is gonna see to it
Curtain up, light the lights
We got nothing to hit but the heights

I can tell, wait and see
There's the bell, follow me
And nothing's gonna stop us
'til we're through
Honey everything's coming up
Roses and daffodils

Everything's coming up
Sunshine and Santa Claus
Everything's gonna be
Bright lights and lollipops
Everything's coming up roses
For me and for you

We sang at the top of our lungs. Dad was right beside me, and I twirled and flung out both arms. I felt big and powerful, and I overflowed with joy. My Dad and I—we really could do anything!

When the record was over, we would not speak for fear the spell might break. Instead, we remained frozen as the room filled once more with silence. Dad seemed to shrink as he returned to his mystery novel, and I glided out of the living room, the music carrying me like wings. For that hour, we had been suspended in time. We became the show, and "there's no business like show business."

When my father died at 61, he was too young, and it was too soon. I was a young woman by then and a parent myself. I asked a friend to sing "Sunrise Sunset" at his funeral. It was the same song he played for me at my wedding.

Is this the little girl I carried
Is this the little boy at play
I don't remember growing older
When did they?
When did she get to be a beauty
When did he grow to be so tall?

Wasn't it yesterday when they were small
Sunrise, sunset, sunrise, sunset
Swiftly fly the years
One season following another
Laden with happiness and tears

The tears still come every time I listen to that one from *Fiddler on the Roof*. Yes, he passed on his love of show tunes, but it took me a long time to understand the full extent of his gift to me. Now years later, wouldn't you know it, I am standing in front of the CD player with my two grandchildren. We just saw *Annie*, and the three of us are singing for all we're worth.

The sun will come out tomorrow
Bet your bottom dollar
That tomorrow, there'll be sun

14

Just thinkin' about tomorrow
Clears away the cobwebs
And the sorrow til there's none

When I'm stuck with a day
That's gray, and lonely
I just stick out my chin
And grin, and say

The sun'll come out tomorrow
So ya gotta hang on til tomorrow
Come what may

Tomorrow! Tomorrow!
I love ya tomorrow!
You're always a day away!

Thanks, Dad. I got this one!

Taming the Dragon

We called her the Dragon Lady, but never, ever, to her face. This was back before Puff, the magic one, cast dragons into a whole new pastel light. Our dragon was the sharp-clawed, fire-breathing kind. We kids never knew when our mother would roast us in a viperous stream of molten flame, tear us with claws, or meet us with a plate of freshly baked chocolate chip cookies. Many were the days when I opened the back door with a whisper to my brothers—*BM*. This was not an endearment and not a reference to bodily functions, but rather a warning meaning Bad Mood. I am not sure who first provided the label, but I would have to guess it was my older brother Steven, since he generally led the way in defensive Mom-action. As the second oldest and only daughter, I took on the impossible role of peacemaker or dragon tamer. I guess it could have been worse. We were an intact family with a home, vacations, and often laughter. But like the lab monkeys who never know when the next electric shock will be delivered, we lived in a state of constant fear.

Magazines and books seem to overflow with heartwarming articles about baby boomers and their aging parents: *A Mother's Love,* or *A Chance to Give Back.* Why don't I ever see the ones titled *Caring for the Dragon* or *Do I Have To?* Am I the only one who does not feel all warm and fuzzy when it comes to the woman who birthed me? I am not sure if I ever liked her. I know I have lived more than half a decade without wanting to be anywhere near my mother. But guess what? A few years ago, I went to Florida and moved her to a beautiful apartment right nearby. But wait, I am getting ahead of my story.

My mother, a brilliant, accomplished woman, was a rager. Just like the little girl with the curl in the middle of her forehead, when Mom was good she was very, very good. But when she was bad, she was awful, even dangerous. We never knew which side would appear, but we became experts at divination. When she was on the rampage, the very air seemed to take on a metallic edge—thin and sharp like fingernails on a blackboard. For two or more weeks at a time, she would be the perfect mom. In a tailored shirtwaist dress, she managed the needs of a busy household and my father's dental practice. President of the PTA, founder of the local Planned Parenthood, competent nurse, and founding Temple member were a few of her many accomplishments. She dressed us, drove us, cleaned, cooked, volunteered, and entertained. She was a one-woman phenomenon. Then the wind (or the brain chemicals) would change. We had little warning and fewer explanations, but we knew when the monster was unleashed. *Get out of the way,* we would whisper to each other.

Once set in motion, the tornado had to run its course; no amount of defensive action could change it. The screams and insults would eventually end in a dramatic, suicidal retreat to her bedroom where she would remain, silent and unwashed, in the shade-drawn darkness for days. Picture me as a shy, knobby-kneed 11-year-old girl balancing a tea cup and plate of toast as I climbed the stairs with dread. I'd walk down the hall to the dank cave—oh, I mean *master bedroom* — where I'd knock tentatively on the door. Opening it, I'd peer into the gloom trying not to breathe in the foul air. "Mommy," I'd whisper, "I brought you some tea." The sodden lump in the bed that was my mother, with her greasy hair mashed flat on her head like scales, responded by rolling over in silence. I'd flinch, place the sacrificial offering on the bedside table, and tiptoe out to safety without daring an over-the-shoulder glance.

If it were today, my mother might be prescribed Seroquel or Abilify with a diagnosis of bipolar or borderline personality disorder: manic highs and depressive lows, unstable relationships, abandonment issues, suicidal gestures, affective instability, and inappropriate anger. It is all there in the DSM-IV. Maybe she'd find a good therapist who would explain her illness to the family. But for us kids, it was simply the family secret and the natural order of things.

We all worked together to contain it and ride it out, but sometimes, like a frozen pipe, it sprung serious leaks. There was the hot summer day when Denise, my best friend forever, and I went to the movie theater. Mom came to get us, but she thought it was the other mother's turn to drive. Mom attacked Mrs. A. with a cold, white fury. I was never able to see Denise again; her mother refused to have anything to do with us. All of us kids were helpless witnesses of these attacks on shoe salesmen, cashiers, and waitresses. There were many people in our small community who never spoke to my mother again after being unsuspecting recipients of one of her scathing outbreaks. Her children didn't have that option.

Steven received the brunt of Mom's fury. Being more tuned in or perhaps more devious, I was often able to avoid it, keep a low profile, stay at a friend's house, and be a "good girl." Steven would have none of that. He faced her head on. They had shouting and

18

pushing matches as often as some families say their prayers. He was endlessly punished and frequently locked out of the house, waking me with the patter of stones on my windows. His pitching expertise was legendary: a mere inch to the left was the dragon's den, too soft a throw and the sound did not pierce my dreams, too hard and the window would break. I would sneak down the stairs to let him in. There were other days when he slept in the woods across the street. As soon as he graduated high school, he left home almost never to return.

We all adored our Dad. He was a quiet, honest, hardworking man who was helpless when it came to his wife. He hated the emotional scenes he was dragged into at home, at his own dental office and every time his relatives came to town. He would slump outside the latest scene of explosion, fragile and mortified. The tension between my parents expanded as time passed, until, at 60, he told me, "I can't live with her, and I can't live without her." A year later, he was dead. The autopsy was unable to reveal any cause of death. But I knew it was his only way out.

When it came to my father's parents and brothers, the rages came with inevitable predictability at weddings, birthdays, and bar mitzvahs. Eventually, our family became persona non-grata, and my quiet father cut off all ties with his beloved parents and brothers rather than put him and them through the agony.

But I loved my grandmother, and from the moment I was old enough, I took the Greyhound bus alone on the 200-mile journey to New York City to see her. My grandparents would meet me at the Port Authority. Today you could not send an 8-year-old alone on a bus, but at the time, I was so proud of my independence. To my embarrassment, my Grandmother would give the bus driver one dollar to look after me on the homeward journey. As I boarded the return bus clutching a bag of cheese blintzes and chocolate marshmallow cookies, she would warn me not to talk to any strangers. Despite my enduring love of Grandma, I always sat down next to someone who soon became my new, fascinating friend. Perhaps that is where my love of travel began. And my Grandmother's steadfast, approving love for me was a glorious lifesaver.

My siblings and I often wondered why no one ever came to our rescue. Even an acknowledgement of the "problem" would have given us encouragement. The few times we dared to describe the latest incident, it was assumed we were exaggerating or outright lying. Neighbors, shopkeepers, waiters, once exposed to her anger, never approached again, while others pretended not to see. Years later, Phyllis, a close family friend, apologized to us. "I should have done something," she said. As we became teenagers, my mother grew more desperate to control us. Our phone calls were tapped, mail opened, drawers searched, and journals read. I became well schooled in lying, sneaking, and evasion. The outbreaks of fury increased in number and intensity as Mom's power over us lessened and her depression increased.

I have grown children of my own now, and I've lived much longer out of my mother's house than those 20 years when I was at her mercy. Now that she lives nearby, I pay her bills, oversee her daily care, do her laundry, clean her toilet, and bring her to my house for Sunday brunch and family dinners. Before you imagine me as a saint, let me explain. The Dragon Lady has

20

become a pussycat— a purring, cuddly one—declawed and defanged. Though my brothers are slow to believe it, I keep saying, "Really, she's harmless."

You see, Mom has dementia. Besides the stacks of unpaid bills, the first sign of change was her lack of combativeness. In that old fire-breathing style, she would stridently announce, "There's something I need to talk to you about." *Uh-oh,* I would think, *here goes.* Long pause—"but I forget what it is." Gone is the extensive, 60-year list of grudges and wrongs that, until recently, she could articulate in great detail. GONE. As if a magic wand transformed her into dear little Puff. In the place of these dramatic stories, there appears to be, for maybe the first time in her 84 years, contentment. She is glad to see me when I arrive, and miracles of miracles, she is fine when I leave. There are no lectures about my shortcomings as a daughter or the way she is being treated or what we kids used to call "the never-enough syndrome." If I disappear for two weeks, she doesn't seem to notice. If I forget to get her bananas, she will tell me, over and over, that she really likes fruit. If I ask her if she enjoyed the concert, she pauses and shrugs her shoulders.

Yes, there is some irony here. All those bitter memories and hurts —she has forgotten them. But where do mine go? I always wanted her to acknowledge her wrongdoings and show us some heartfelt regret. Instead, I find that I am missing the Dragon Lady. After all, she was my dragon. I never knew what would meet me, but there was a morbid fascination with the unknown menace. The many cozy hours my brothers and I spent sharing mommy-dearest horror stories gave us strength, a mutual hardiness, and an unbreakable bond. I used to daydream about a loving, gentle mother,

21

but perhaps I would have found her unbearable. This new, passive, old lady is unrelentingly dull. In the good old days, Mom would scream, "What were you thinking?!" after she saw footprints across the hood of her car or caught my brothers perched high in a tree surrounded by a haze of smoke. Now I want to ask her, "What are you thinking—are there any thoughts at all?" I believe it was Bernie Siegel who said, "Meanness and anger cause illness." Not for my mother. Aside from the dementia, she has nary a health issue; she is still as strong as a dragon. But there is an ironic lack of nobility in a declawed, defanged dragon. It becomes a cartoon character, something more like Mr. Magoo.

Lately, I find myself with a tiny, creeping tenderness for Mom. She is so helpless. It is a bit like the feeling I have for an injured bird. Will I miss her when she's gone? Not likely. Recently, I asked her why she had so many bitter fights with her children and relatives. She looked at me, all sweet innocence, and said, "What fights?" "You don't remember being mad at your son, your brothers-in-law, your neighbors?" I asked more directly. "No-o," she said, surprised. What could I say? "Do you want mushrooms in your omelet, Mom?"

Earth in Balance

It is the autumn equinox. Days and nights are the same length, and fall is officially here. Of course, if you are like me, you are more likely to notice that you are out of milk or that your son's room is an unholy mess. But most of us have observed that the days are growing shorter, right? And we all have felt the chill in the air.

The last hurrah is being dramatically proclaimed in my garden: the clown-like pumpkins have grown triumphantly large, the crimson tomatoes are pungent and rotting, and my flowers are crumbling into seed pods. It seems that everything is dying until I look more closely and see the seeds. They are everywhere; acorns are lining squirrels' nests, burrs are hitching rides, and sunflowers are filled with spiraling bounty. The promise of new life is here side by side with death. Maybe that is what the earth in balance means. Life and death all goes together.

This is the time of Michaelmas, when St. Michael, leading the host of angels, rushed in to battle the dragon and drive him out of heaven. With his lance, Michael pinned the fire–breathing monster down to earth and saved us from evil. I sure hope he is on duty this year! In Waldorf schools, this is a celebration of inner strength and courage where children practice facing their challenges, their internal and external dragons. Will the sword of righteousness prevail?

In the Jewish faith, it is the celebration of the Days of Awe. Here is the birthday of the universe, the day God created Adam and Eve. It's the time when our fate hangs in the balance as God reviews our past year, and decides whether or not to renew our lease on the planet, and if our names will be transcribed in the Book of Life. By performing acts of repentance, prayer, and good deeds, you can change your decree until Yom Kippur, the Day of Atonement, when the book is sealed. Then you must live the life you have made for another year. After almost 6,000 years of practice, there is bound to be a clue about balance there.

In my daily life, I find balance to be a rather challenging concept. Let me give you an example: last week, I was rushing. This is nothing unusual, but this particular day started off wrong. I slept through my meditation, spilled a glass of orange juice, and found my office keys had gone missing. At work, an appointment was double-scheduled, and to top it off, I had dressed for the morning chill, and by mid-day, it was already hot. I was bedraggled and discouraged — definitely NOT balanced.

I should listen to the Buddhists. They believe in The Middle Way, the Eightfold Path, and celebrate equality and inner harmony at the equinox. The Eightfold Path is Right Understanding, Right Intent, Right Speech, Right Action, Right Livelihood, Right Effort, Right Mindfulness, and Right Concentration. These are some darn good rights. The monk Kawabe says, "The time between darkness and light is the time when all Buddhas attain Buddhahood." Reportedly, this time often occurs on the equinox. Count me in!

Let's look at Eid al-Adha, an Islamic festival in September that commemorates the willingness of Ibrahim (Abraham) to follow Allah's (God's) command to sacrifice his son Ishmael. As Ibrahim was about to sacrifice his son, Allah stopped him and gave him a sheep to kill in place of his son. To commemorate God's test of Ibrahim, many Muslim families sacrifice an animal and share the meat with the poor. They also donate to charities that benefit the poor. Muslims around the world observe this event every fall.

It somehow comforts me that people from so many places and faiths are celebrating in similar ways. The earth's rotations are, after all, universal. What is the key for me in all this? How do I balance work and family demands with my own need for exercise, rest, and solitude? How do I dedicate myself to meaningful work, scrub toilets, chauffeur kids, create a healthy dinner, and then turn into a love goddess by bedtime?

It reminds me of fourth grade recess when I was on the seesaw suspended in mid-air. My best friend Joanne and I had gotten it just right, perched exactly evenly, and it felt so good. I raised my hands up triumphantly and let out a whoop. But even at that moment of exultation, I knew it was over. I would soon be thrust high in the sky clinging precariously to the handlebar or, even worse, ignobly dropped down to the dusty earth. What I didn't know then was how little things would change more than 40 years later. I am still on a seesaw searching for that precious feeling of balance, which remains brief and elusive.

So, it is important that I take a moment to breathe deeply and exult in our mother earth's equinox as she hangs so exquisitely in the balance. If I go forth into battle armed with prayers and good deeds, perhaps my personal dragons will be stilled and some of the earth's balance will rub off on me. Maybe by eliminating some fear and frenzy and welcoming loving kindness and contentment, I can perch once more on the seesaw of life. This time I'll be sure to take in the view, knowing it will not last for long.

Yogi Tea Recipe

There is no better offering to the Goddess of Balance than this tea! In India, it is sometimes called Spice tea. We enjoyed it often when we lived in the ashram. Good almost anytime, it is especially welcome on a dark, cold winter morning. Assemble it the night before, bring it to a boil, and then turn it off and cover it. Go to bed. It will be waiting to comfort you in the morning.

Most recently, we had it when the extended family gathered after a sorrowful memorial service for my brother Peter. I can't think of anything more soothing than family members sharing stories and Chai/Yogi tea, even in the wake of sadness.

Each of its ingredients is said to have healing properties:

- **Black pepper** is a blood purifier that improves digestion
- **Cardamom pods** are good for digestion and combat nausea, acidity, bloating, gas, heartburn, loss of appetite, and constipation.
- **Cloves** benefit the nervous system and have antioxidant, antiseptic, anti-inflammatory, and anti-flatulent properties.
- **Cinnamon** strengthens the bones and combats nausea, acidity, gas, heartburn, loss of appetite, and constipation.
- **Ginger root:** is healing for colds and flu, increases energy, is great for women's cramps and for colds, and has anti-inflammatory, antibacterial, antiviral, antioxidant, and anti-parasitic properties.

When you get Chai/Yogi tea in a coffee shop or use prepared tea bags, it is not the same; those contain oils and flavorings, and are usually too sweet. Try making it from scratch. Here is my recipe guideline. I say guideline because no one I know ever made Chai by measuring ingredients. Just throw a handful of this and that in. You can't go wrong!

Ingredients:

- 6-10 green cardamom pods
- 12 cloves
- 2 cinnamon sticks
- ½ to 1 inch ginger root, sliced thinly
- 1/4 tsp black peppercorns
- 1 or 2 tea bags of black or decaf black tea
- 7 to 12 cups water
- Milk according to your preference
- Honey to taste before serving

Preparation:
1. Bring the water and spices to a simmer for 15 or 20 minutes.
2. Add the tea bags, and let sit for a few minutes.
3. Then add the milk (almond milk may be substituted) and heat again, but do not boil.
4. Remove the tea from the heat and sweeten it with honey, if desired. I do not even strain it. If an ingredient or two finds its way into your cup, you will know it is authentic Chai/Yogi tea!

5. Hold your mug with two hands and breathe in the aroma. You feel more peaceful and centered already, don't you?

I usually drink half or more of the tea and then refill the pot with water and return it to a simmer. You can get at least two complete servings out of the initial ingredients. Sometimes my pot of tea seems to continue on indefinitely like the magic porridge pot in the Grimm's fairytale.

We are Stardust

I woke in the morning light to a panorama of dust and blowing debris. My neck ached, and I was covered in mud from sleeping on the ground. I was hungry and smelly too, but all that was instantly forgotten. The morning silence was suddenly shattered—*Oh say can you see, by the dawn's early light*. Up on the stage, a tall, skinny man wearing a fringed shirt and a red bandana around his Afro was doing things with his guitar that should be impossible. It took me a few minutes to remember where I was. Woodstock!

> *We are stardust*
> *We are golden*
> *And we've got to get ourselves*
> *Back to the garden*

It was the summer of 1969. Lee and I were barely old enough to vote. All summer we worked: me in Boston and he on Long Island. We heard whispers about a music festival in the Catskills and Lee quickly ordered tickets. That Friday we rendezvoused at my parents' house in Saratoga Springs, loaded his car with a new mini tent, sleeping bags, a few clothes, some food, and a box of chocolate chip cookies. Wearing my newly sewn, Indian-bedspread mini dress with long, flowing sleeves, I jumped in and we set off.

About an hour south, we exited the thruway into traffic that soon slowed to a complete halt. Gridlock! The hillside was strewn with vehicles as if they had been dropped from above like Pick-up Sticks. We added our car to the collection and joined a river of humanity all walking in the same direction. There were so many people, mostly young, in all sorts of dress or undress. We had been called hippies before, but our hippie membership was soon put in question by these elaborately fringed, beaded, long-haired, and practically naked enthusiasts. There were people laughing, calling, singing, ecstatic twirlers, stoned zombies, tie-dye clad babies, decorated animals, and painted buses. It was an amazing scene!

Here's what else made this a once upon a time fairytale. Almost exactly a month before, like almost everyone in the United States of America, I was sitting in front of a little black and white television watching Neil Armstrong and Buzz Aldrin land the Apollo 11 on the moon. We all worshipped the moon that Sunday as Armstrong stepped onto the lunar surface on July 21, 1969. With mouths agape, we listened to his voice coming from 240,000 miles away as he spoke these words to billions of people listening at home: "That's one small step for a man, one giant leap for mankind." After lumbering back to the Lunar Module, it then landed in the Sea of Tranquility. It truly was a time of tranquility as people all over the world rejoiced to see what humankind was capable of achieving.

There was something so '50's-confident and optimistic about that moment in time. Little did we know it was the last awe-inspired unity we would see maybe ever again. But the Apollo missions were actually the culmination of a massive, competitive arms race between the USA and the USSR that resulted in the first rockets capable of striking across the world. The moon was an excuse to gain greater control. This is what led Eisenhower to warn against the "military industrial complex", a term he coined. In 1966, less than three years before that celebrated walk on the moon, NASA received its highest budget ever, the equivalent in today's economy of $43 billion. Here was the connection we suspected between the race to the moon and the current war in Vietnam.

And now, on a Friday afternoon only three weeks later, we approached the entrance to a festival in the town of White Lake. Lee was wearing his backpack and clutching our precious tickets in hand—two of less than 50,000 tickets sold at $18 dollars apiece. There was a scuffle just ahead of us. As we watched, the tall fence was ripped down, and the crowd surged forward, stepping on top of the chain link fence as if it was the road to Oz. It was done. From that moment forward, the festival was free and open to one and all. We tossed our tickets to the wind and joined the bright flow.

I didn't know where to rest my eyes. There were day-glo tableaus everywhere, signs to read, naked bodies to appreciate, and a sea of service booths: lost and found, first aid, food stands, bad trip tents. Announcements such as I'd never heard before blared over the loudspeakers—*The brown acid is bad. Do not take the brown acid. Mary Louise please go to the information booth. Seth wants to marry you. Ron, your wife is having a baby.* And people, people, people everywhere! Not all the same but, at least for that weekend, all like-minded and big-hearted.

A bit overwhelmed, we decided to set our backpack under a tree while we headed off into the crush to explore. Soon we found a comfortable spot on the sloping hill overlooking the stage where we waited for the music to begin.

Eventually, Richie Havens strode onto the sun-drenched stage in socks and sandals and a long, orange caftan. "Hey lookie yonder, tell me, what's that you see?" Richie sang, strumming his guitar in time with the bongo player. He closed his set with an amazing 20-minute version of "Freedom," which he later explained had been made up to fill the time until another performer arrived. He quickly earned a place in our hearts.

Of course we loved Swami Satchidinanda, a little holy man from India with orange robes and a long white flowing beard unlike anything we had ever seen. We didn't know then that later we would study in his beautiful Yogaville Center in Virginia. "My Beloved Brothers and Sisters," he said greeting the crowd. "I am overwhelmed with joy to see the entire youth of America gathered here in the name of the fine art of music. In fact, through the music, we can work wonders. Through that sacred art of music, let us find peace that will pervade all over the globe." Who knew, but it sounded right to me! Then he led us all in our first chant ever: *Hari OM Hari OM, Hari Hari Hari OM.*

Even the heavens were full of enthusiasm. The skies opened with thunder, lightning, and a downpour. Stagehands rushed to secure instruments while the audience simply got wet. No problem. Some people removed their already skimpy clothing and, after a while, played in the mud while most of us just laughed and waited for the sun to dry us and the music to resume.

Later that night, after Joan Baez sang "Oh Happy Day" under the star-studded sky, we returned to the tree to gather our tent and backpack only to discover that our things were gone! Life does seem to present us with these forks in the road. Did we freak out? Get angry? Go home? No. Instead we decided right there that it was not in the spirit of Woodstock to freak out. And that is when we truly became stardust. Light, unencumbered, and trusting in this magical universe, we forged ahead; just us, the clothes on our backs, and our love for this new world.

We hiked back to sleep in the car for the night. That station wagon was spacious and dry, complete with an old blanket, and, wonder of wonders, a box of chocolate chip cookies. The universe does indeed provide!

When most people think about Woodstock, they imagine the music and the astounding lineup of bands. And it was fantastic; it was the soundtrack to our lives that launched the careers of Santana, Crosby, Stills and Nash, Richie Havens, and Joe Cocker. Sometimes we even think of the few who did not appear and soon regretted it: The Rolling Stones, Bob Dylan, and The Doors, who later admitted they were stupid for not coming.

But, I think for most of us who were there, it was only peripherally about the music. We reveled in it, of course, and danced to it, and even slept to it. But Woodstock was every day, every hour, every minute about the overwhelming sensory experience of being there in community with others and knowing we were part of a life-changing experience.

Standing in the mud, in the middle of a seething group of joyful people as far as the eye could see, we were sure that the world had shifted. In this city of half a million, despite the sun, rain, mud, and the lack of food, water, and comfort of any kind, there were almost no outbursts, fights, violence, or serious problems. This was a new world that would be led by peace loving hippies who would end the war, by Michael Lang, the young, brash co-creator of the festival. It would be led by Wavy Gravy, the founder of the Hog Farm Commune and The Phurst Church of Phun who came to the festival to feed people. Dressed in his usual clown clothes, he greeted the sleeping bodies Saturday morning with, "We must be in heaven man!" The trumpet sounded Taps, and he announced, "Breakfast in bed for 400,000!" It all signaled the dawning of a new world.

The New York Times did not want to report on the festival. Barnard Collier, a young New York Times reporter, was turned down by editors and publishers who believed the festival was not newsworthy. But he went anyway. When the traffic forced highway closings, he asked his editors again, and they reluctantly agreed. Stepping into a completely empty press trailer, he soon realized that it was not only The Times that had initially ignored the event. There was a virtual news white-out as all the mainstream press remained mostly silent. But he proceeded to write several articles over the next few days, including one where he explained recreational drug use to his mostly uninformed readers. He also quoted many older area residents who commented on the extraordinary peacefulness of this unprecedented gathering.

Soon John Sebastian was on stage. He looked around and said, "This is really a mind fucker!" before he sang:

> And hey pop, my girlfriend's only three
> She's got her own videophone
> And she's taking LSD

He came to an abrupt halt because he was too stoned to remember the lyrics. It didn't faze him in the least. With a little help from the audience, he finished.

And now that we're best friends
She wants to give a bit to me
But what's the matter daddy
How come you're turning green
Can it be that you
Can't live up to your dreams?

On the final day of the weekend, a *New York Times* editorial denounced the whole event saying, "The dreams of marijuana and rock music that drew 300,000 fans and hippies to the Catskills had little more sanity than the impulses that drive the lemmings to march to their deaths in the sea." Though it reluctantly added, "the great bulk of freakish-looking intruders behaved astonishingly well."

Rolling Stone, more in tune with young people, said it better: "A new nation has emerged into the glare provided by the open-mouthed media." Woodstock is now acknowledged as the starting point for modern music journalism and was the first time real attention was given to youth movements.

I remember being perched on the hillside after the early rain, looking out at the colorful, seething sea of people and hearing Country Joe McDonald leading our resounding chorus of voices in, "1,2,3 what are we fighting for? Don't ask me, I don't give a damn, Next stop is VietNam." And I was thinking, *will we do it? Will we build a world worth living in, a world safe for children?*

Saturday night we found ourselves, at dusk, on the far shore of White Lake. A swim seemed the perfect antidote to the mud and sweat of the past 24 hours. We slipped surreptitiously out of our clothes. Despite being

36

a child of Woodstock, I was, and still am, rather shy, so I attempted to go unnoticed as I glided into the delightful embrace of cool water. We swam out into the center of the lake and looked back to shore in time to see some guy bending over the little pile of clothing — *our clothing!* Those clothes were all that was left of our earthly possessions. I quickly imagined spending the rest of the weekend utterly naked. Lee yelled out, and the guy said, "Oh sorry," and strolled away. And that, my friends, is how it came to pass that I did NOT dance naked at Woodstock!

> *By the time we got to Woodstock*
> *We were half a million strong*
> *And everywhere*
> *There was song and celebration*
> *And I dreamed I saw the bombers*
> *Riding shotgun in the sky*
> *And they were turning into butterflies*
> *Above our nation*
>
> Joni Mitchell

Wedding Vows

Pomona, California

It was the morning of my wedding, a day that is supposed to be one of romance and joy; the most important day of my life.

I woke up on the floor of a large room in Pomona, California, crammed with scruffy, sleeping bodies. Lee, my on-again-off-again boyfriend, rolled his sleeping bag towards me and whispered tonelessly in my ear, "I don't want to marry you. I am not sure I even like you." There was a moment of panic—*oh no, he doesn't want me*—and then I remembered that I didn't really care; marriage was his idea.

"What about all the people who stayed up most of the night preparing a wedding feast?" I asked. Typical me; instead of being concerned about being chained to the wrong man for the next 50 years, I was worried about what people would think.

Rochester, New York

Lee and I met early in my freshman year of college. We went on one unmemorable date and then did not speak or interact again for the next 18 months. But that is a story for another day. After Lee graduated and I dropped out of school, we bounced around together and apart. We had agonized breakups: he cried, and I turned to stone. We had passionate reunions. Finally we called it quits. Done. Over. Goodbye and good riddance. He drove off, hurt and angry, in our powder-blue Opel Kadett. I headed to Vermont with some vague notion of a commune where I would grow potatoes and live an enlightened life. I was a free woman.

Almost New York City

The commune idea quickly went up in a cloud of hashish smoke, so I decided to head to California. I found a ride advertised in the *Village Voice*. His name was Ray, and he was going to take me to meet my friend Angela who was living in an ashram in San Rafael. She was always doing interesting things, and I was fresh out of ideas. Ray and I spoke a few times by phone. I asked him if there were any other passengers coming with us to share the driving and expenses. I did not want to be alone in the car with this unknown man. He reassured me there would be two or three others.

New York City

I met Ray in front of Alexander's on Queens Boulevard. My heart sank when I saw him slouched against a beat-up Chevy in a black fishnet shirt with copious chest hairs poking through. I asked about the other riders. "They dropped out at the last minute," he said. I knew he was lying. My friend Debbie urged me to cancel out of it. "Take a bus, or wait, don't go." I got in the car. We drove and drove and drove. Every time he wanted to stop, I insisted we keep going. When he was tired, I offered to drive. When we were both beat, I suggested we pull over and nap or pick up a hitchhiker.

Nebraska

We got as far as North Platte, Nebraska. Geography was never my strong suit, and Nebraska became confused with Nevada, so I was thrilled that we were already in the west. *Couldn't be far now!* Turned out I was only 1,900 miles off. Darkness spread like a blindfold, and the lovely autumn rain turned into a torrential downpour. Ray, who was already grumpy, became dangerously angry. After a few miles, he screeched a sharp turn into a neon-lit motel, stormed into the office, and checked us in. I quietly followed him in to room 301. What was I thinking?

A few hours later, I was alone in a hotel room, my things strewn in the dark puddles of the parking lot, and all the money in my wallet gone. I was lucky. Really. He only pushed me around, took my cash, and then left me in the pre-paid hotel room. I was okay. Really, I was. After sobbing loud and long, I checked all my pockets and came up with a folded twenty-dollar bill, a few singles, and some change. I called the bus station to see if I could get to Berkeley with my twenty dollars. No such luck. So I went to sleep in my paid hotel room. What else could I do?

When I awoke, the sun was shining, and my hopefulness had hatched like a golden Easter chick. I would have to hitchhike. Not my first choice, but the only one that seemed possible. I slung my pack on my back and hiked back to the highway. I stood there with my thumb out and watched one dusty pickup truck after another slow and then pass me by. Every single one of those trucks had a rifle in the back window. I wasn't in New York anymore. Then I saw it, coming out of the highway haze, a green VW bug! A VW bug in Nebraska! Either I was hallucinating or my luck was returning. An older man, maybe all of 35, pulls over and asks if I need a ride. He was going to San Francisco!!!! This apple green apparition in Nebraska was heading west. California, here I come!!

San Rafael, California

I joined Angela in a crumbling Victorian mansion-turned-ashram that was channeling better days like an old British dowager late for tea. After my cross-country experience, I was ready for a convent, but an ashram just might suffice. I threw myself into a celibate and simple lifestyle. Meditation began at 5 AM, and yoga was three times a day followed by karma yoga. I chopped wood, carried water, and cleaned the kitchen. Sore, achy, and content, it felt as if I was doing something that mattered. This was Kundalini Yoga as taught by Yogi Bhajan, who had recently arrived in the country and was somewhere in Los Angeles. For three weeks, I only left the house to walk around the neighborhood or do an errand with other ashram members. I was becoming a recluse. But one day, I decided to go into San Francisco for new contact lenses.

San Francisco, California

After my lens acquisition, I dropped in on the only person I knew in San Francisco—Peter. He was not overjoyed to see me and seemed nervous. Barely half an hour after I arrived, Lee walked in the door. What?? I had no idea where he was, and he thought I was harvesting potatoes in Vermont. "Come with me," he romantically implored. I told him about my path of yoga and meditation. I was immersed in it, and it felt important. Turns out, he had been practicing the same teachings of Yogi Bhajan with folks in the Redwoods. This was a cosmic zinger. You can't write fiction this far out. Of all the gin joints in all the towns in all the world, we found the same spiritual path with the same teacher and then re-found each other. This was too powerful to ignore, even if you didn't believe in Karma or destiny.

A week later, I was tucked into the blue Opal following on the tail of an overloaded logging truck winding my way north.

"Where are we going to live?" I asked.

"You'll see," he sweetly replied, "I fixed it up for you." Upon arrival, Lee proudly displayed my new home. I was not expecting fancy. Honestly. I can make do. But a hollowed-out redwood stump?? Well, it was actually two stumps facing each other with a blue tarp stretched across for the roof. There was a shelf for our things and padding for our sleeping bags. It was not getting a write-up in *Architectural Digest* nor would it pass any inspection, but I wish I could show you the view down the ridgeline.

We did yoga and meditation every morning in a geodesic dome with two other couples. One couple lived in the dome, one in a teepee. We cooked meals in a little half-trailer. I am not kidding! During the day, we worked on the land, and once a week at dusk, we drove along the winding road, where deer and elk leapt out onto our path, to a hot public shower.

One afternoon, I was placed up on Daisy, the passive horse. Clumping along — trot, gallop, canter— across the canyons with magnificent, queenly trees, feral, long-horned sheep, an expanse of sky racing the Douglas firs to the end of the world, I was the Marlboro man. Life couldn't get more perfect.

Out, out bright spot! Amid all this pastoral beauty, two things happened:

1. Rain. Cold rain. Picture our redwood stumps as the rain peeled down the hillside to pool into our sleeping bags.
2. Lee and I began fighting again.

One beautiful California day, we were out digging ditches—yup—like a chain gang without the chains or the singing, or even speaking, when Lee threw down his axe and yelled, "I've had it!" *Well this is it,* I thought. *At last I got him so angry he is leaving, or more likely, kicking me out.*

Instead, he explained that we had tried everything, and the only thing left was to get married! What?? That's your solution to 'I've had it?' He seemed to think it was, so we agreed to go to LA where Yogi Bhajan was teaching a 10-day tantric yoga retreat (no, not the kind with sex). We would ask him to marry us. I wasn't worried. I knew he would say no when he saw what a mess we were. We had heard that this often happened. But I really wanted to meet this Yogi, so two weeks later, we were on our way back down the Pacific coast.

Pomona, California

And that is how I ended up slumped hopelessly on the floor the morning of my wedding. Two days before, we called and invited our East Coast parents to the wedding. They were, needless to say, horrified. My parents thought that Lee was a terrible influence on me, and Lee's parents were sure I had dragged him into a cult. So neither of them came, and I don't think either of them believed it was a REAL wedding. By the time I was dressed in a tablecloth from the Salvation Army that I had sewed into a wedding dress, I had a terrible stomachache. I was so nervous. Yogi Bhajan was surely going to interrupt the ceremony and embarrass me. He had been known to send couples away, telling them that they were not ready for the commitment. I was convinced that he would see the sham that was our relationship. And yet, somehow, we were soon married and eating delicious, homemade ice cream. People said it was the most mellow wedding that Yogi Bhajan had ever performed. I don't know. To this day, I can barely tell you what we did or he said, but he must have seen something that we could not yet discern. After all, it is 40 years later, and we are still married. We haven't slept on any floors lately, but let me tell you about our latest adventure. It involves bicycles and boats.

And when at last I find you
Your song will fill the air
Sing it loud so I can hear you
Make it easy to be near you
For the things you do endear you to me
Oh, you know I will
I will

The Beatles

Challah Recipe

My youngest child Avi was getting married. Rosaly had said yes!! And they were getting married in our backyard in early June. What a blessing! High on the list of preparations was to bake Challah.

That spring, after two sessions of intensive challah baking we placed 14 loaves in our neighbor's freezer to await the wedding day. On that day, each table was given a challah along with butter and salt. We were braiding two families together with a blessing to guide these young people on their way.

I started baking bread early in my motherhood years. It was a wonderful pastime that was both satisfying and delicious. My children often joined in with their own portion of dough to flavor and shape. We had circles and spirals, women and soldiers and dragons. They looked out at the world with raisin eyes, cinnamon hearts and honeyed souls. When we resolved to keep the Friday night Sabbath, I learned to bake challah.

Challah is a special bread, eaten on ceremonial occasions. According to Jewish tradition, the loaf commemorates the manna that fell from the heavens when the Israelites wandered in the desert after fleeing from Pharaoh's army.

In the tradition of the Sabbath meal the blessing is said over the bread: "*Baruch atah Adonai, eloheinu melech ha'olam, hamotzi lechem min ha'aretz*" or "Blessed are you, Lord, King of the Universe, who brings forth bread from the earth".

Though it takes some time, Challah is not difficult to make and the satisfaction level is indeed high. If you have any leftovers you can make the most kick-ass French toast for breakfast!

Challah Recipe For 2 loaves

(with partial thanks to Joan Nathan and the NY Times)

- 1 packages active dry yeast (1 tablespoons)
- 1 tablespoon plus 1/2 cup honey
- ½ cup vegetable oil, more for greasing bowl
- 5 large eggs
- 1 tablespoon salt
- 8 to 8 ½ cups all-purpose flour
- Poppy and/ or sesame seeds for sprinkling

Preparation

1. In a large bowl, dissolve yeast and 1 tablespoon honey in 1 3/4 cups lukewarm water.

2. Whisk oil into yeast; beat in 4 eggs, one at a time, with remaining honey and salt. Gradually add flour. When dough holds together, it is ready for kneading.

3. Turn dough onto a floured surface and knead until smooth. Clean out bowl and grease it, then return dough to bowl. Cover with plastic wrap and a dish towel, and let rise in a warm place for 1 hour, until almost doubled in size. I often use the warmed oven because my house is cold.

Punch down dough, cover and let rise again for another half-hour.

4. To make a 6-braid challah, either straight or circular, take half the dough and form it into 6 balls. I make three larger and three a little smaller. With your hands, roll each ball into a strand about 12 inches long and 1 1/2 inches wide. Place the big 3 in a row, parallel to one another. Pinch the tops of the strands together and braid. Tuck the ends under. Take the smaller three balls and braid. Lay on top. Make a second loaf the same way. Place braided loaves on a greased cookie sheet with at least 2 inches in between.

5. Beat remaining egg and brush it on loaves. Let rise for 35 or 40 minutes.

6. Preheat oven to 375 degrees and brush loaves again. Sprinkle poppy or sesame seeds onto each loaf.

7. Bake in middle of oven for 35 to 40 minutes, or until golden. Cool loaves on a rack.

The Wonder of It All

To see a world in a grain of sand
and heaven in a wild flower
Hold infinity in the palm of your hand
and eternity in an hour
William Blake

When I urge parents to fill their children's world with wonder, someone inevitably asks, "But what about preparing them for the real world?" I picture a greenhouse. If we grow plants in a warm, supportive environment with lots of sunshine, predictable temperatures, perfect moisture, and good nutrients, then strong, deep roots systems develop, the leaves grow green and bushy, and the plants are soon covered in blossoms. It is no surprise that the term "nursery" is used for both plants and young children. The first 6 years of our children's lives are their greenhouse years. They receive the warmth of our love, the moisture of our tears and laughter, the control of our discipline. We never forget to feed our children—indeed, most of us watch their diets rather closely—but the nutrients that create the blossoms are often overlooked. These nutrients are make-believe and wonder. They create the final touch of beauty, the glow of contentment, the peace of reverence.

My family has come to believe in unicorns, elves, and fairies. It was not an inherited belief. I started out as a skeptic. What use would I have for such things? I am a busy, practical woman intent on accomplishing many things in a day. However, I soon discovered that our frenetic world of scientific truth, specialties in every field, computer programming, and live news coverage leaves little room for wonder—a quality of life that young children thrive on. Having seen the demonstrable effects of the imaginative life, my husband and I now assume the enjoyable responsibility of coaxing wonder into our family life.

Our 3-year-old would wake up screaming that a lion was in her room. We tried to convince her that it was a friendly lion. She remained terrified. We changed tactics: no lion would be able to come to our house. This reasoning also offered no comfort. Finally we explained that our two cats would guard her, and with her help, we arranged the stuffed animals around her bed as additional protection. She heaved a great sigh of relief and went to sleep. The nightmares ended.

The following suggestions will help you create a world of wonder in your home. If you have trouble relating to elves, try to stay in the realm of nature.

Following the Seasons

Spring. What greater magic is there than a sprouting seed, a crocus in the snow, or an apple tree decked out in pale pink like a princess? During spring cleaning, tell the story of Mother Earth waking all her elves and bugs to clean and paint the blossoms. It can transform the drudgery of doing chores into the joy of being busy elf assistants.

Summer. Magic reigns supreme during these hot and hazy days. Remember Puck's mischief on a midsummer's eve? Catch a glimpse of a hummingbird, grow a pumpkin, watch the waves eat a sand castle, or wonder of wonders, be blessed by the sight of a rainbow.

One summer evening, we were gazing out over a field covered with fireflies. "Look at the fairies dancing," I exclaimed. My middle daughter, our realist, answered, "Those are fireflies, Mom." Our older son hastened to explain that they were fairy lights until they were captured by people, at which time they instantly become fireflies.

Autumn. At a time of death comes the promise of renewal. Seeds are everywhere—a reminder of continuity. The countryside is filled with the wonder of the harvest, of the falling leaves, and of the ripe, rosy apples.

We knew a 4-year-old who had lost all his hair. The scientific reasons for his hair loss had been explained repeatedly by his doctor and his parents. Around Halloween, my daughter asked him why he had no hair. He replied matter-of-factly, "The monster took it." And he skipped off. This explanation was to-the-point, made more sense, and was actually comforting to this child.

Winter. In the old days, this was a time to slow down and mend our nets. Although we are no longer forced to slow our pace, doing so can transform our experience of the holidays. Winter holidays lend themselves easily to a sense of wonder, for they involve the kindling of light to illuminate the outer darkness.

In our family, the stuffed animals traditionally disappear the week before Christmas. They go to help Santa's elves. On Christmas Eve, we return from a snowy, song-filled walk to discover the house glowing with candlelight (a friend does service as our resident helper-elf). We are welcomed by the stuffed animals. Repaired and cleaned, they are decked out in new scarves, jackets, or ties. The children see the candlelight in the windows and run in shouting, 'The elves have come!" They greet each animal. "Cucumber has a new dress!" "Look at monkey's patched tail!" This is one of life's special moments.

When my older children began asking if I was the one who had done those things, I explained that the elves are extremely shy these days, and we needed to help them out. The older children were then happy to join in the fun from the other side, acting as elf assistants for younger siblings.

Giving to the Elves

Children enjoy giving gifts. Sometimes they have an ulterior motive in hoping for a gift in return. Nevertheless, they engage in the giving. They may make a tiny loaf of bread, or draw a miniature picture, or sew a tiny sleeping bag. My son once created a row of miniature hats, each one of a different type and all fashioned out of colored beeswax. The children like to leave these gifts in a special place for the elves.

Receiving Gifts from the Elves

Keep it simple. Little gifts are best: a dried pineapple, an acorn, a few chocolate chips, a new sticker. What excitement those can produce! One time, my husband and I drew tiny, one-inch square storybooks for each child. Another time, late at night, I arranged a new set of wooden animals surrounded by pine boughs on the girls' floor. The breathless morning discovery is much more satisfying then "handing over" a gift. A bureau might be neatened in the night and bordered with dandelions. A mysterious card might arrive in the mail. It is incredible that those elves know how much we all like to receive letters.

Telling Stories

Make up little stories while you are cooking, weeding, or driving. They can be about elves and fairies, nature and weather, or your own childhood adventures. Young children are amazed by reminiscences and anecdotes of their parents as children. "Mommy, tell the one about your broken leg." "Tell about the time your mommy yelled at you."

On long trips, we sometimes do a pass-along story. One person begins, and after a few moments, he or she stops and the next one continues, and so on. As the excitement mounts, my youngest child is usually too involved in the listening to do any more telling until the final turn. "They lived happily ever after. The end."

Creating Together-Time

In these busy, overscheduled times, unstructured time together is essential and can be enhanced by wonder. Consider adding wonder to the many "non-activities" that occur in the course of a day: reading aloud, cuddling, giggling, playing silly games, singling together, taking walks. Some of our best talks and strongest connections have come during our after-dinner walks.

The important point is to find the things that help you enjoy each other and share in the joy of life. Slowing down just enough to enjoy the miracles in the world will go a long way toward enhancing life. Find the way that works for you, experiment. When you see the expression of joy in those young eyes looking up to you, I guarantee you will be convinced.

If the nourishment of imagination comes during the early, receptive years of childhood, it will form a foundation of love, self-confidence and creativity that the children can draw on for the rest of their lives. So, go ahead, give the world of wonder a chance. Then wait and see; the elves will weave their spell over you!

All in the Family Granola Recipe

Is there anyone who has not eaten granola? It is everywhere. Some people love it and have a favorite brand; others think it all tastes like toasted cardboard. You can get it in the cereal aisle, in the health food store, or in the high-end bakery downtown. You can get it with almonds or Brazil nuts or pecans. You can get it vegan or made with powdered milk. You can get it organic or gluten free or simply natural. The choices proliferate.

But I remember when granola was kind of new; when it marked me as the hippie that I was. I can't recall exactly when I started making my own granola but it was sometime after Woodstock and before I had child number two. In those days, you didn't buy it, you made it. I started making it for my family and I have been making it ever since.

Granola seems to have been introduced or created in the USA at the end of the 19th century when it was considered a health food alternative. Look at this wonderful add. It claims that one pound of granola is the equivalency of three pounds of beef. I am not sure if this means the equal in protein, or energy, or health, but I am pretty sure that most of us do not intend to eat either one pound of granola or 3 pounds of beef at one sitting.

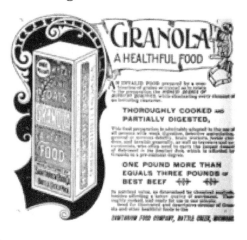

Although there was a small contingent of odd health nut adherents eating a dull, dry form of granola, it was not until it became the signature food of the hippies at the end of the 1960's that it really began to gain momentum. Today there are hundreds of brands of granola and new ones coming out every day. But who buys granola? In my family, we make our own. My mother-in –law makes it, my sister-in laws make it. My son makes it. And all these years later, every few weeks, I make it.

However our family has an even more intriguing connection to granola. In 2010 my sister in law, Jody, launched Boulder Granola with the tagline, *Unleash your inner hippie.*

Boulder Granola's Head Hippie.

Yes, that really is Jody and that van really does exist!! Boulder Granola truly is one of the best ready-made granolas out there. Many of my nieces and nephews sold granola at the Farmer's Market and the product made its way into Whole Foods and other markets. Look for it.

But if, like me, you prefer to make your own granola, here's the way I do it.

Ingredients

- 4 cups old-fashioned oats, use the thick variety if available
- ½ cup almonds, chopped
- ½ cup walnuts, chopped
- ¼ cup pepitas (green pumpkin seeds)
- ½ cup sunflower seeds
- ¼ cup sesame seeds
- ¼ cup of powdered milk, if wanted
- 1 teaspoon ground cinnamon
- ½ teaspoon sea salt
- Scant ½ cup maple syrup
- Scant ½ cup melted coconut oil or canola oil

Preparation:

1. Preheat the oven to 300 degrees Fahrenheit

2. In a large mixing bowl, combine the oats, nuts and seeds, cinnamon, and salt. In a liquid measuring cup, whisk together the maple syrup, vanilla and coconut oil until combined. Pour the wet mixture into the dry, and mix well.

3. Transfer the granola to the prepared baking sheet and use the back of a big spoon or spatula to spread it out and press it down.

4. Bake for 35 to 40 minutes, rotating the pan halfway through, until golden and fragrant. Let the pan cool completely to keep the clumps intact. Gently pour it into an airtight container. It will keep at room temperature for at least 3 weeks (or for several months in the freezer).

Possible additions:

Add coconut flakes (I like the big thick variety). If you add it add it halfway through baking it will be a little toasted but it is good raw, too.

Add flax seed whole with the oats or ground after it is baked.

Any dried fruits can be added after the granola is cooled. Dried cherries, dried cranberries or chopped dried apricots are all delicious.

Use certified gluten-free oats if you need gluten-free granola.

I store it in a half-gallon canning jar, but any airtight container will do.

B♥ULDER
GRANOLA

UNLEASH YOUR INNER HIPPIE™

Clockwise from Top Left: Mom and Dad.
Glassman family 1961. Arnold Glassman
1982. Laura Rose 1963.

Top: Wedding 1972.
Bottom: Elves at play; Avi and Julian.

STEMS

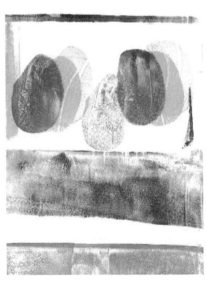

Winter Sustenance

Back when Gerald Ford was president, but before he pardoned Nixon, I was the specials chef at a popular restaurant. My training: I knew how to read a cookbook, and I showed up. Also, I was clueless enough to believe it was possible. When I think back on it now, I wonder how we did it. I remember one day, our mixer was not working, and so I offered to make the whipped cream for the day's dessert in the blender instead. Seems possible, right? Not wanting the cream to turn into butter, I opened the lid to check on its progress. Unfortunately, the blender was still going. Whipped cream soared up to the ceiling covering everything in a fluffy white perimeter! If only that was my worst mistake.

The restaurant was the Golden Temple on DuPont Circle in Washington, DC. It was named after the Golden Temple in Amritsar, India, the holiest place for Sikhs. This was when Lee and I were members of 3HO, following the teachings of Yogi Bhajan. Like Brigadoon, the restaurant seemed to rise magically out of the fog, and after a few years, it was gone.

That was an enchanted time, and in some small way, we knew it. Lee and I lived in a crumbling brownstone on Q Street with many others. We were in the master bedroom where we slept on a mattress on the floor dwarfed by six-foot windows that we could not afford to drape. Our room included a small alcove that we set up as the nursery for our 18-month-old son Moses.

Just when we thought we were getting the parenthood thing figured out, we were asked to take on a second son—let's call him Rami—who was the same age as Moses. It was an informal foster care agreement. We were suddenly the parents of twins. If we weren't careful, we would have our own baseball team in a few more months.

Every Sunday, I would pick up the boys from the basement ashram day care, and we would walk to the restaurant for community dinner. Five city blocks should be an easy stroll. Only most days, it took us almost an hour to get there. Little Rami had decided that he could protest his destiny with two forms of passive resistance. One was a vow of silence. He had tapped into a long, noble tradition passed down from Thomas Merton to Meher Baba. So while Moses was chattering on with new word discoveries every day, Rami had carefully selected a single word as the essence of his little life: "NO". He practiced that word with one-pointed concentration. His second method of resistance was a refusal to walk. Poor guy, he had already learned passive resistance. It took Gandhi many years to fully understand that lesson.

Slowly, slowly we would make our way to the restaurant. I spent the entire walk trying not to explode in utter frustration. For someone who likes to keep moving, this was the ultimate torture, and Rami seemed to relish my frustration. I would count to ten to keep from screaming. I do not remember the return walk, but I think by then we caved and carried him home.

But let's get back to the Golden Temple Restaurant. Vegetarian restaurants were a very rare sight in those days, and the few that existed were old, dingy, unimaginative places or joyless kosher establishments. The Golden Temple was absolutely beautiful. There was soft lighting, melodic chants playing, and white-turbaned young servers. Customers came out of curiosity, but many came back again and again for the food. I wonder if we would think the food was good now that we have all become such gourmet snobs, but in my memory it is absolutely delicious.

One of my favorite specials from those days was what we called Bhajan's Banquet, named after our teacher. He recommended this as a cure for run-down health and for women after childbirth. The ingredients made it a high-protein, but easily digestible meal. If you ask me, it is good almost anytime. It is still one of my family's favorite meals. Nothing is better for a cold winter night. Check out the recipe.

Bhajan's Banquet Recipe

     This is the full-protein, warm-you-up, easy-to-make winter meal you could order long ago in DC. It is really quite easy to make. The vegetables are all interchangeable; use what you like and what is available. Then you can spice it more or less depending on your palette. I use a rice cooker, but a slow cooker works too. I suggest you sauté the veggies in a frying pan (cast iron is the best) before adding them to the mix.

Ingredients

- 1 cup short grain brown rice
- 3/4 cup mung beans
- 5 cups water
- 1 tablespoon oil
- 2 stalks celery, chopped
- 1 carrot, chopped
- 2 onions, chopped
- 1 bell pepper
- 1 cup of broccoli in medium florets
- ½ cup kale, de-spined and cut in pieces
- 1 jar or can of whole tomatoes, optional
- 2 cloves garlic, minced
- 3/4 teaspoon coriander
- 1 teaspoon turmeric
- 1 teaspoon ground cumin
- 1/2 teaspoon mustard powder
- 1/4 cup soy sauce
- dash of black pepper cayenne pepper to your preference and/or grated cheddar cheese

Preparation
1. Wash the beans and rice.
2. Combine with water in a saucepan or, even better, in a rice cooker with a little salt and cook for 45 minutes until the beans begin to soften and pop.

3. Meanwhile sauté the vegetables in the oil until tender. Use any combination of vegetables. Sometimes I use some tomatoes. And beets can help the dish take on a cheerful red hue. Winter squash is also lovely.
4. Add the spices to the vegetables and simmer until the beans are done.
5. Combine the vegetables and the beans and cook 15 minutes.
6. Place in a dish and melt the cheese over the top.
7. Sprinkle some gomasio (sesame salt) and cilantro on top if you wish.
8. Add hot sauce if desired.
9. Serve hot with a fresh salad and some warm nan or bread. Yum!

Angels in Residence

Three dozen small children clutch the handles of elaborate paper lanterns created out of their own colorful watercolor paintings. Bundled up against the early snow, we wind along the path singing, "Lanterne Lanterne, Sonne, Mond und Sterne." The little ones are mesmerized by the shimmering light that spills into the frigid night, and as I gaze behind me at the winding procession of dark forms, each a sparkling diamond of light, I, too, feel the enchantment.

The lantern walk, a European tradition, is a testimonial to the light. Though the light outside fades as we approach the winter solstice in December, the ceremony is a promise that the light will once again return. Meanwhile we must keep the glow within.

This is the Spring Hill Waldorf School. I began the school in 1980 for Kiara and 11 other nursery students on the upper floor of a small synagogue in Saratoga Springs. It was more than a school, it was a family. We celebrated, suffered, and grew together: teachers, children, parents, and even grandparents. My children grew up in the classrooms and halls sharing their toys and furniture and napping on the teacher's room rug as interminable faculty meetings drew to a close. Almost every year, we added a grade. I started out teaching preschool and kindergarten then later, 1st and 2nd grade. I chaired the board for ten years. Today the school encompasses preschool through 12th grade, has 300 students, owns three buildings, and exerts a significant influence in our community. Many children have passed through its halls on their way to adulthood.

Looking back, I wonder how I found the chutzpa to start a Waldorf school. It took more energy than any of my children. I was even warned against it by some of the higher-ups in Anthroposophy. They thought the school would fail in provincial Saratoga Springs. My founder's tale goes back to 1972 when Lee and I and our baby Moses moved to College Park, Maryland. Moses was 9 months old, and Lee was starting clinical psychology graduate school at the University of Maryland. We had been part of Yogi Bhajan's 3HO community for a few years practicing Kundalini yoga and meditation, dressing all in white, wearing turbans, and attempting to live a righteous life. So when we moved to Maryland, we began to teach a yoga class at the university that became very popular.

The next fall, I registered at the University of Maryland to take a few courses towards finishing my long-stalled undergraduate degree. Soon our dedicated yoga students were telling me about an honors course I should take. Western Esoterisism was taught by Clopper Almon, an erudite economics professor. The class was named to sound like a normal college offering, but this was no normal course. It was a crash course in the teachings of Rudolf Steiner. For those of you who do not know, Rudolf Steiner was an Austrian spiritual leader, scientist, artist, and prolific writer who died in 1925. Out of his impressive body of teachings came Waldorf Education, biodynamic farming, eurhythmy (a form of movement), architecture, art, meditation, Camp Hills (for people with disability), and much more. There are now more than 1,000 Waldorf schools in 60 countries and China is adding a few new ones every year.

I was a 24-year-old new mother struggling to figure out the rest of my life. I knew I was committed to following the teachings of Yogi Bhajan and raising my son, but was sure of little else.

Then along came this class with Clopper, and I was thrust deep into the readings of Rudolf Steiner. I don't know if you have ever read any Steiner, but there are hundreds of books to choose from, and they all have one thing in common: they are dense and difficult. So there I was in an afternoon class in an overheated classroom for three interminable hours discussing the etheric body. I had awakened for a 5 AM meditation practice, taken care of my toddler, and had to go right to work in the ashram restaurant after school. I sat listening to a brilliant professor drone on about a dead Austrian man. Can you guess what happened? I fell asleep in class. Every time! So, as you can imagine, I was none too thrilled. But near the end of the class, I went up to Dr. Almon and asked him, "So this Steiner guy, did he have anything to say about education?

The rest, as they say, is history. The next semester Dr. Almon guided me through an independent study on Waldorf education and gave me a personal introduction to the kindergarten teacher at the Washington Waldorf School. It was, at that time, located in the magnificent National Cathedral. When I stepped into that classroom filled with flowing rose-colored silks, soft, handmade dolls, and worn wooden blocks, I was flooded with the wonderful sense of coming home. This is where I wanted to be, where my children belonged. This is where the world was set right. A year later, I started a master's degree in Waldorf education.

Waldorf education overflows with magical stories. The teaching in each grade is based on stories. First grade uses fairy tales, second grade is Aesop's fables, and later classes move into Norse myths and historical biographies for history and science. As I became a practiced storyteller, the magic wove its charms into my psyche. All the arts filled my life along with the students'. Recorder playing, knitting, painting, drama, and singing became everyday events. Waldorf Education gave me so many things, but the gift of wonder stands out. Though we never forget to feed our children or put them into a warm coat when the temperature drops, we sometimes overlook wonder, imagination, and dreams. Waldorf education is based on wonder.

The education became more than a school philosophy to us... it modulated, and still does, so many ways that we see the world. The teachings are deeply pertinent to our world today and important to the growth of whole human beings. It still amazes me how many of Steiner's indications seem spot on 100 years later; like the importance of the arts, not as short detours in the week but woven in as an integral part of the entire curriculum. All children are artists, and there is a natural development process in children that should not be rushed in order to nurture the artist within. There is an understanding of the important role played by nature and the need to keep young children free of screens and media.

Steiner explained that each of us is a body, soul and spirit. Waldorf pedagogy emphasizes the role of imagination in learning and strives to holistically integrate the intellectual, the practical and the artistic development of the students. There are three stages:

73

young children need to be protected in order to first play and experience a reverence for the world as a good place to live. The focus is on practical, hands-on experience and creative play. Walk into a Waldorf kindergarten and you will see children singing and baking and playing in a beautiful panorama of wood and silk and comfort. Reading is not taught until after a child is 6 years old.

In the lower grades, the focus is on the development of artistic and social experiences so that the children have a chance to see the world as a place of beauty. In high school students explore truth through dynamic thinking using critical reasoning combined with empathy-filled understanding. They come to experience what is true based on personal experience, thinking, and judgment. We want to give them, not specific facts that may soon change, but capacity. Quantitative and standardized tests are not found in a Waldorf school. Neither are textbooks. In 1st through 12th grade, children make their own textbooks called Main Lesson books. They are filled with beautiful text and colorful pictures derived from the main lesson work. Many of them look like the illuminated textbooks of the Middle Ages.

Our highest endeavor must be to develop free human beings who are able of themselves to impart purpose and direction to their lives. The need for imagination, a sense of truth, and a feeling of responsibility—these three forces are the very nerve of education.
Rudolf Steiner

On the day I was rushing to City Hall to register the school as a new business, a few of us stood on the steps of the Temple looking out at the view down the bluff towards one of the many springs in Saratoga Springs. That view is now obscured by the city center, but at the time, it offered a fine vista. When deciding what to call the school, we tried out various names until Lee suggested Spring Hill School. And thus, it was done. Spring Hill School of Saratoga Springs was officially born. Twenty years later, the new chairman of the board came to me for permission to change the name to The Waldorf School of Saratoga Springs.

After many years of struggling to find a home for the school and the money to buy it while renting various spaces, we purchased the neighborhood brick school building. This was the same school where I attended kindergarten and 1st grade many years ago! For the previous ten years, it had been used by a contractor to store supplies. With Herculean effort, parents and faculty cleaned it out and began renovations.

Six months later, I sat in our newly purchased building with a visiting advisor from Detroit. He was a wise, older man with plenty of Waldorf school experience. Spring Hill School was desperately trying to keep afloat. We wanted answers. Where would we get the money for repairs? How could we increase enrollment? Would we find qualified teachers? We bombarded him with questions. Our doubts filled the room, our fears chilled the air. He looked at us and said, "When you start an endeavor that is for the children, you call the angels down. I can feel them. They are here."

In 2016, 36 years after our quiet beginning in Temple Sinai and 10 years after his high school graduation from the Waldorf School, my son Avi was invited to speak at the high school graduation. He was but a sparkle in the firmament at the time the school began, but he was coming. He is the only one of my children able to attend the school from nursery through high school. As he stood at the podium in his dark suit, just arrived from his job in New York City, looking confident, kind, and oh-so-handsome, I had to stop gazing proudly at him for just a moment and give a little thank you to Clopper Almon for putting up with a yawning skeptic all those years ago. Yes, the angels are here!

A Creation Story

Time: Hot day in august

Place: Upstate NY

Characters: 2 women, 3 young children,
             1 grandfather, 1 doctor, 1 father

Scene 1: Garden, late morning

The August sun presses down on my bent back like a hot waffle iron. Sweat trickles between my heavy breasts as I pick ripe tomatoes from my very first garden. It is August 25th. Like the tomatoes, I, too, am swollen and ripe. Today is my due date.

Six weeks ago, we purchased an old farmhouse with its surrounding acres. It is our dream come true. My husband Lee and I settled in with Moses, our 4-year-old son, and after distributing our meager furnishings throughout the house with a liberal sprinkling of pillows and Indian bedspreads, we managed to clear a small garden and plant vegetables. Despite the idyllic location, the house is undoubtedly haunted. The creaks and moans sometimes wake us.

Lee's internship continues on Long Island until the end of the summer, and so every Monday morning, he departs at 4:30 AM not to return to us until Friday evening, leaving me and little Moses to battle the bats, mice, and ghosts alone. Today is his last day there. He is coming home to a new job beginning after Labor Day. My friend Pat and her two little girls have come from Boston to keep me company for this last week. This morning, I urged her, "Go, I know how much you have

77

to do in your own new house before school starts. Lee will be here soon, and I'm fine." But she refused to leave me until Lee arrives that evening.

The three children, rosy and sun-kissed from a morning at the pond, are napping. The tomatoes fill my basket. Suddenly, I double over with the full force of a contraction. *Uh- oh.* Is this it? Now? After an hour, we've decided that I am, indeed, in labor. We call Lee. Just heading for his farewell party, he shouts his goodbyes, throws his things in the car and gets on the road. We call my doctor. Four years ago, before Lee and I moved away to go to school, we birthed Moses at home with the gentle assistance of Dr. C. As far as we are concerned, it is the only way to go. I want to welcome my children in the comfort and privacy of my own home, and we were so lucky to find a doctor who is willing to work with us. There is one catch: If Dr. C is in the hospital attending a birth; he will be unable to come to our house. When Pat calls his office, we are told that we must go to the hospital. *No Lee and no home birth? No way!* This hits me like a disaster. I am literally stunned and horrified. I don't even have a bag packed. Very slowly, I pull myself together.

"Remember," Pat reminds me, "What really matters is that this baby arrives safe and sound." That's right, I want to meet this new one, and the rest is just background. I throw some things into a bag, call my father to come and babysit for the sleeping children, and we head out.

Scene 2: The car, early afternoon

Dad arrives looking a little dazed by the speed of this new development. He was none too pleased with the whole home-birth nonsense, so he approves this

78

new plan—*Yes, go to the hospital and have a baby like a civilized person.*

Pat drives as I hunch over in the passenger seat wracked by increasingly strong contractions. Steering with one hand, she rubs the pain in my lower back with the other. Every time I catch my breath, I look up and give directions. The seven-mile trip, like a dreamtime, stretches and contorts. My field of vision narrows to the road directly ahead and the coming contraction.

Scene 3: The Hospital; afternoon

We park and clamber in through the main entrance right up to the front desk.

"Where is Dr. C?" I practically scream.

"He is not here," the receptionist replies.

"He must be," I pant, "Check the delivery room."

Just as she checks, the other phone rings. It is Dr. C's assistant in his office, "He is here. Come to the office."

If I had entered through the emergency room as I was meant to, I would already be admitted, so instead, I do an about-face and waddle out the front door. People are shocked. How many overripe, pregnant women, clearly in advanced stages of labor *leave* the hospital? Pausing only long enough to sit on the front steps for the next contraction, we load once more into our little VW and take off. Pat is honking as she drives through red lights. We race into the waiting room where patients in various stages of belly expansion wave me through. Dr. C examines me.

"You are nine centimeters dilated," he says, "Go home. I am right behind you."

Nine centimeters! This mobile distraction may be a new state-of-the-art labor technique. I have been so busy, so distracted, that my labor has progressed practically unnoticed.

Scene 4: That d%#* car again.

 We arrive back home much to my father's shock and dismay. I am still carrying a baby in my womb. He looks a bit panicked at the idea of being more involved in this drama than planned. He definitely did not sign up to see his daughter give birth. Pat hustles him and the rumpled, sleepy children out to his car. "Go. Take them to the park or anywhere." Meanwhile I go around the back to avoid conversation. I have my next contraction with my head in the grass.

 Once they are gone, I race up the stairs, tearing off my dress as I go. I have never been so happy to see my bed. With the very next contraction, my water breaks to the sound of Dr. C's arrival and a calm voice saying, "Go ahead and push." Two or three strong pushes and there is a baby between my legs! Just as I am trying to catch my breath, Lee comes pounding up the stairs. He made it home in record time.

 "If only I did not stop for gas," he exclaims as he greets his daughter. Daughter! It's a girl. A girl!! I have all brothers and one son, so I never pictured myself with a daughter. What a miracle.

 Lee cuts the cord and hands her to me. She is perfect. I place her to my breast as Dr. C says it is too soon for her to nurse. She latches on with noisy, contented gulps. Her name is Kiara, and she is already a wonder.

 An hour later, my son and Pat's daughters return with my father. I am nervous about Moses' reaction because, all along, he has been saying that he wants a brother whom we should name Risky Rob. But in excitement, he says, "I was only fooling, I really wanted a sister!"

We have a BIRTH-day celebration complete with a cake (taken out of the freezer at the first sign of labor) and a little present for each child. What a way to bless our new home. Lee is here to stay. It is indeed home sweet home. And there are plenty of fresh, sun-kissed tomatoes for everyone.

How does this story end? They lived happily ever after? Well, I am not so sure about that, but we're pretty good for now.

My Son the Street Person

Let me start off by confessing: my son lives on the streets. I don't say this easily. Of course, in response to a casual inquiry about him, I usually say, "He's doing great." If pressed further, I say, "He's traveling." No one can fault that. After all, many restless young men spend a year roaming before they settle down and go to college. They need to get it out of their systems, sow their wild oats and find themselves. But questioners may remember that this is his second year out of high school. How many wild oats has he got?

Most of the interrogators let it drop. They are too busy with their own life dramas. Or perhaps they feel an inky darkness lurking beneath my terse answers, a darkness they want to avoid. But some people are tenacious. "Where is he?" they want to know. A tale of international intrigue and foreign languages is on the tip of my tongue, but for some reason, I am compelled to tell the truth, so I answer, "New York City." I hear the wheels turning. How long can you be traveling in New York City? There are a lot of sights, a few good day trips, but, hey, two weeks ought to do it. A huge writhing can of worms gapes open until someone finally asks, "What's he doing? Where is he living? How is he supporting himself?"

"My son is a street person," I finally admit. I glimpse the shocked response before it is stuffed away and then the oozing, obsequious, "Why?"

And then they quickly change the subject. It's as if my son were dead.

The sociological data on street kids is extensive; it says they typically come from divorced, alcoholic, abusive, unloving, uneducated families. While that's the classic profile, it's not an accurate portrait of my son or our family. My husband Lee and I have, amazingly enough, been married for 21 years. We've never enjoyed alcohol, and despite my genteel attempts to cultivate the pleasure of a glass of wine now and then, I must admit, the stuff puts me to sleep. We reprimanded our son and sent him to his room on occasion, even grounded him once or twice. But he was an easy child and, in our family, yelling is something you do on the sidelines of a soccer game. We tend to talk things out or make silent assumptions. Unloved? This child has been adored, admired, enjoyed, and cherished since he was conceived. To this day, he lights up a room when he walks in. There is a zest for life that can't be missed. So please don't say it is lack of love. I did not do everything right each day of the past 19 years, but love him? That I did. This kid's so smart; his high school teachers still talk about him. Education is a deeply running stream on both sides of the family. Our family tree is practically sprouting with doctors, lawyers and teachers.

Having eliminated all the usual criteria of homelessness, "mentally unbalanced" is the only one left. He must be crazy, right? Wrong. He's the most rational, practical person you could hope to meet.

My son has lived on the streets for more than a year now. He is not homeless or living out of a cardboard box. He is a squatter, living with a group of people in an abandoned building that is city-owned. This is not without precedent. Street people take up residency, begin repairs, and do their best to avoid authorities. Others link in, and soon there is a community of sorts, with rules, guidelines for joining and extended support for older, neighboring squats.

In the beginning, I imagined he was planning to write a book or an article, or make film to document the squatter lifestyle. Or I thought he was going to organize assistance programs for the homeless. I had it all worked out. My son: the social activist, the do-gooder. But it turns out that he did not go to New York City to *help* those "poor people." He just wants to be, to live. In fact, he claims, any other way would be a form of manipulation, taking advantage of street people, standing apart, and observing. He is living his life. Though he comes home for occasional visits, he does not ask us for any money or help.

My son has *chosen* this life. I have to keep reminding myself that he is not there because he failed. It is not a last resort, a desperate attempt to survive, a dead end. He wants to be exactly where he is, and he's happy about it. Nor did he do this out of some romanticized notion of what it would be like. He's tried it out in NYC, San Francisco, St. Thomas, and Seattle. He knows the hunger, the fear, the loneliness, the violence, the disease out there. He is not a romantic idler; this is an informed choice.

Day after day, I ask myself why. Why did he end up in this place, in this predicament? I will never be able to fully understand or accept it. I cannot change it, approve of it, or even explain it. Yet it doesn't go away. That is my child out there. I have talked to many of his friends. Upon overcoming my initial reaction to body piercings, ripped and smelly clothes, and dyed and shaved hair, I find them to be kind, intelligent, thoughtful people. They are all searching for something.

84

After my initial horror, I began to comprehend some of the appeal of this life he has chosen. It is a day-to-day existence in which there is no worry about career goals, bills, what your neighbors think, or even entertainment. These squatters focus on the basics of survival. How am I going to eat today? Where will I sleep? How will I keep warm? Where will I relieve myself? These are questions that inspire considerable passion and take up a major portion of each day. After these are settled, a squatter is free to pursue his or her own thoughts and daydreams. There is, indeed, a freedom in the squats. The price is danger, discomfort, bugs, and ill health; the street beats you up and ages you quickly. But the freedom is there. It is not pretty, pastel, or romantic, but beneath the dirt and the desperation, I can sometimes see it through my son's eyes.

A strong sense of community exists among his friends. There are a few sub-groups: the down and out families who are there as a last option, the drug dealers and users, the desperate young runaways, and the others like my son, who are there by choice. Some are old-timers; others are new to the life. The group my son is part of has organized their places of shelter into a network of communication that could be a model for any activist group. Within minutes, a hundred people can be mobilized to come to the assistance of others. There is an excitement and purpose in their rejection of a world order they consider to be decadent and wrong; no one here is abusing the earth, taking advantage of people, or accumulating wealth. They may be more certain of what they do not want than what they do, but in their view, they do no harm.

They live in buildings abandoned by society, eat the food that is thrown away in vast quantities, and scrounge for clothing and furniture from discarded piles left on the curbstone. Books on revolution and philosophy are passed around and discussed late into the night. They offer each other protection and assistance, often giving their last dollar to one whose need is greater. They are proud of their ability to survive! Sometimes I think they are teaching us about the dysfunction in this nation of unhappy, out-of-control, futile consumers.

I do know the dangers of his life. On long nights when fear grabs hold of me and will not let go, I see them clearly. I imagine all those guns in New York City; I see berserk crack heads or aggressive dealers pursuing him. I picture him caught in crossfire, poking his head in the wrong dumpster, or simply ticking off some hothead. I see him cold and shivering, dirty and lice-covered, sick, his immune system weakened, and diseases ready to ambush him. I see him falling in love and wanting to settle down but unprepared for a "normal" life. I see these things, and for all my attempts at understanding, I am simply a frightened mother.

My endless ruminations fall away and are replaced by excited anticipation when he returns for a visit. The one form of assistance, other than spare building supplies, that he accepts, is an occasional roundtrip bus ticket home. We cook a big meal, stock up on fresh baked bread and Jarlsberg cheese, and stay up late listening to his descriptions of the people in his life: the local hot dog vendor who sees everything, the Puerto Rican brothers who own the bodega, the corner drug dealer, the young couple from Ohio, the artist with AIDs, the old communist who has been living like this

86

for 25 years, and the old guy who taught my son how to do plumbing so he could hook the squat into the city water main—they all have a story.

"Explain your reasons to me again," I entreat. "This time, perhaps, I'll understand." We talk. I hear a young man who is committed to something, who is excited, learning, and changing. These are good signs.

In the daylight, I surreptitiously examine his skin sores, listen to his cough, and check out his cuts and bruises. He plays with his little brother, takes his sisters out for coffee, and repairs our shower.

The local grapevine carries word of his arrival in town. By the second evening, a jam session is underway in the back room, the pulsating bass notes lulling me into a contented sleep.

What is the price he will pay for this lifestyle? I don't know, though I try to guess. I do know that he is young and his goals will change (though the college graduate we once imagined is a dream long deferred). I am much clearer about my cost: the endless days of worry, the incessant wondering about what we could have done differently, the hesitant greeting I give him while I look at the sores on his face with a growing dread. Yet is this so different from any parent? I may think my case is more dramatic and extreme, but in the end, we mothers all worry and pray for our children whatever their age or whereabouts. Our inability to insure safety and happiness never changes the longing.

Yes, I feel embarrassed chagrin when I am questioned, and sometimes I believe I am the failed parent others perceive me to be. Yet I am also proud. This handsome, vibrant young man to whom I gave birth has found the courage to take control of his life. He is on a quest, even if its goal is not a golden chalice.

He is learning, seeking, and questioning everything. What will be his future? What will be the future of his world? In the old days, he might have gone west of searched for a river's source; today the cities have become our wilderness. Perhaps he, more than me in my frenetic, practical life, has found what it is all about. Who can say for sure?

Postscript. One bitter cold day in February two years ago, shortly after I jotted down the words you've been reading, the entire community of squatters was forcibly and violently evicted without their clothes, a blanket, or a place to sleep. My son, the group's spokesperson and mediator, was the only person arrested.

During our 8 year-old son's birthday party, we received a call telling us that he was somewhere in the New York City jails. He remained there, unreachable, for three days. Even though officers at various police desks around the city repeatedly assured us that he could not be in jail since they could legally hold him for only 24 hours, he was confined for 72. We were told that Mayor Giuliani wanted to send him to Rikers Island as a lesson to all squatters.

One year later, after much panic, many tears, and telephone consults, his case was finally resolved. He received a suspended sentence and was assigned to East Village garbage detail for a month (something he rather enjoyed!). We breathed again.

Two years have passed. No longer a teenager, he is working, putting himself through an audio-engineering program in Orlando, Florida, and quoting the *I Ching* about the importance of acceptance and patience. He is enthusiastic, joyful, creative, and still a revolutionary.

Now if you have a minute, can I tell you about my 18-year-old daughter?

Command and Conquer
Written with Avram B. Nagel

There is my teenage son—he just got home. Straight away, he sits in front of the computer, revs up his favorite video game, and becomes a moron. Really. His mouth hangs open, and he hears nothing around him. He does not get hungry nor need a bathroom break. His feet do not fall asleep, and his fingers do not get cramps. He hears me only if I practically stand on top of him, make physical contact bordering on pain, and speak in short, loud sentences.

I would say I am an involved parent. I ask lots of questions. I explore new interests alongside my kids. I tried laser tag and now, with minimal translation, I can decipher a hip-hop message. But I am lost, completely undone, by video games. What is it about these macho contests? They take a bright, young man and turn him into a robot that is, as we speak, entering a trance state at the computer. What's going on? He is, I think, a well-adjusted kid, interested in current events, does his homework, cooks decent pasta, and volunteers to work with children and sea turtles. What's going on?

Avi: *My royally pissed-off mother comes barreling up the stairs towards me. "Get off the computer this instant. I just got back from school, at least it seems that way, and she's already furious with me. I've been playing Madden Football, and I am in a clutch fourth quarter, 3rd and 9 in a playoff against the Ravens. My adrenaline is pumping, and I'm ready to execute a pass to Wayne Chrebit over the middle. I've been stalling my*

Mom since the 2nd quarter. I know the end is near.

Doom, Mortal Kombat, Age of Empires, Grand Theft Auto, Command and Conquer, Halo. I don't know all the names; I do know the games are everywhere. The sounds of screams, crashes, gunshots, and explosions are terrifying. If you stepped into the room, you might think your home is being invaded, or your neighbor is dying a painful, death.

As a parent, I often question the onslaught of media in general and video games in particular. How do I guide my children through this? Some psychologists tell us that electronic games contribute to obsessive and addictive behavior, desensitizing of feelings, health problems, and development of antisocial behavior while others assure us that video games increase coordination and prepare youngsters for the future. Who do we listen to?

Most of our children are now frequent flyers on the information skyways. They start teething on instant messaging and expect new electronic wonders every year. Their thumbs and fingers seem to have evolved to fit onto multi directional joysticks and screens of all types. Many feel the need and, indeed, the right to be connected at all times: texting, talking, Instagramming, and tweeting. Entertainment and relaxation often involve a movie, a video game, or YouTube.

Though I had confronted the TV question with my other children, it was not until child number four that I faced this invasion. I wrestled with the choices, but unfortunately, my response often depended on the moment. Some days I ignore him, taking advantage of his rapt state to do my own things. Other days his zombie demeanor turns me into a raging terror. I yell and rant until I come up with lists of chores, homework, and projects that must be completed immediately. I want to shake some normal boy interests into those glazed eyes. As far as Avi is concerned, he is fully engaged and has no idea what was wrong with his mother.

Avi: *Brian and I are going to John's house to play the new* Grand Theft Auto. *We climb down the basement stairs where we worship at the altar of 21st Century technology—a 32-inch flat screen TV, PlayStation II, and Dolby surround sound speakers. We have hardly stepped in the door and gone through our basic greeting—"hey" and "what's up?"— before Brian scoops up the first person controller lying on the futon, hits the power on the TV, and is off. Chainsaw in hand (so to speak), he begins cutting a Mercedes into pieces. I am next in line. Within seconds, I am a two hundred and fifteen pound African American gangster on the streets of LA. I have a brother in prison, and I work for a nasty drug dealer named Tarnik. This history is written into the game and is mine for the touch of a button.*

In 2000, video games topped $20 billion in sales, and that number has risen dramatically each year since. About 145 million Americans play video games, and although adults are a growing percentage of this number, children remain the largest consumers. The vast majority of the top-selling games contain violent content. Video games are promoted to young people with the zeal and financial power reminiscent of the tobacco industry. We now know for certain that tobacco CEOs knew their product causes cancer, but they managed to keep this information from the public for decades. Like tobacco, video games are BIG business. It is not in their best interest to discover detrimental effects of video games on our children. Therefore, parents must come to their own conclusions and set their own guidelines. It is not easy but there are some actions we, as parents, can take.

Exert Some Control

Remember you are the parent. Yes, I know it's possible in the chaos of life to forget this fact or even to wish you could forget it. But you must be the one in charge. Be alert to inappropriate content, especially in regard to sex and violence. Develop reasonable time constraints and prepare for resistance. It's okay, that's their job; they need something to push up against. These controls can be amended and expanded as your children grow.

Participate

Find occasions to play with your children—not always but sometimes. Notice what they are listening to and playing and get a conversation going. Play stupid and curious. Ask, "How exactly does that work?" or say, "I heard about this new game..." First, try to understand what they like and why, try it, and then share just a little of your reaction.

Check for Developmental Appropriateness

What is right for a toddler is not usually going to work for a teenager. And even more significantly, adult games exert a more profound impact on young, developing brains. We now know that the brain develops different areas at different stages of life. How children, and especially teens, use their time and where they focus their attention is significant to this development. Do some research and make some informed decisions.

Prioritize

What is important to you and to your family? Does your use of time and resources reflect these values? It is likely that you want to place homework, meals and other family time, chores, and exercise and sports first. What comes next? Maybe videogames comes in somewhere with TV and other recreation. Hold a family meeting to negotiate priorities.

Begin to notice how your child feels and acts after playing the games. Point it out to him or her. Research is becoming clearer that there is a cumulative effect of playing violent video games. You know your child best. Does he pick fights after a long session of gaming? Does he withdraw and seem detached from family life? Does she have difficulty focusing on anything else? Pay attention, and you are likely to know if there are problems developing.

Watch for Signs of Addiction

Some signs of addiction and seriously negative impact are: your child's time spent on video games is increasing, he or she becomes increasingly isolated, shows increased anxiety, irritability or belligerence, sadness, or sleeplessness, or their school grades drop. Keep in mind that normal adolescents often exhibit some of these symptoms. They can also indicate other problems such as depression or other addiction issues. Please consult a professional if you see persistent, multiple, or extreme signs.

Keep it in a Central Location

Whatever you do, resist putting a TV or computer in your child's bedroom. Not before the teen years, but even better, not at all. Don't do it. Computer gaming is isolating. If your children are in their own room on their own equipment, there is nothing to keep them connected to you, and you will have lost all control over time and content.

Relax and Enjoy

How are you going to do that with all the worries and dangers lurking out there? Remember they survived teething and *Hooked on Phonics*; they'll survive this too. The best inoculation against video game problems is to build strong family bonds and enjoy each other.

All this video practice must be good for something. My kid has logged enough hours for a merit badge. Does it smooth out the over stimulation of our times? Or does it test his dexterity and determination? Is it a need for extremes, excitement, and violence? Maybe it is a macho thing. Our boys are no longer able to hunt buffalo or ride a bucking bronco. Instead they undergo a virtual reality rite of passage.

Avi: *Instantly I run out of the house, rip an old lady out of a shiny white sports car, and speed away. "Whoa!" John exclaims as I fly over three cars and land on the hood of a truck. My car flips, sparks flying as it careens across the sidewalk flattening two pedestrians and a lamppost just before coming to rest against the wall of a tenement building. The car is still good to go. I may*

95

be hurt, but it doesn't matter. It's the flashing white letters that get my attention: Insane stunt bonus – extra points!

There are so many voices telling Avi what to buy, how to look, and what will feel good. Where are the voices urging him to create a meaningful life, develop caring relationships, heal the earth, and find his higher power?

As in so many things, we come back to moderation. Video games are not in themselves evil. Most healthy children will play video games and grow up to be caring, responsible adults. The older they are before they play violent games, and probably the less they play them, the better. They have other more important things to do like playing outside, reading, conversing with real people, daydreaming, and mowing the lawn.

Avi: *Everyone always asks me, "How can you like this?" I don't play often, but I like it when I do play. Don't worry; there are other activities I enjoy as much. I am just as likely to get a group of guys together to play tackle football in the nearby field. I went through high school without one fight, and I swear I have never participated in any car theft. The only gun I have ever held was my uncle's, and while it was in my hands, I was not consumed by a desire to shoot anything other than the target. So how is it that I can pick up a controller and commit atrocities that would impress Jack the Ripper? It's fun! For a short moment in time, I can do anything: climb eight-foot fences, jump off buildings, steal and flip a car. And most amazingly—no one suffers from it. I have this* *virtual experience, and I do not even have to leave my seat!*

I want my son to grow up with the values and strengths he needs to navigate an uncertain future—one I can only barely imagine. I worry that all the time that video games will stunt his growth, cause him to torture small creatures, or rot his brain stem. The results are not in yet, but thus far he is a kind, thoughtful, gentle young man (if you get him away from the monitor).

I ask him, "Why do you like playing?"

"It feels good" he answers. "It is exciting, but also it is relaxing. You do not have to think about anything. It kinda displaces everything else that might be on your mind."

My nephew adds, "It lets you do things you wouldn't normally do, and you forget about everything else."

It appears that this is their form of mindfulness meditation. Maybe it really does impact the brain waves in a similar way. Why would I ever want to impede that?

So I guess I will have to call a truce: I'll try to ignore the video games if he stops making fun of my Joan Baez albums.

If Wishes were Sisters

All my life I wanted a sister. My mother had a sister, my brothers had a sister, and my best friend had two sisters. If I had a sister, I would brush her hair, share all my clothes, and let her explore my secret place in the woods. Together we might even dare to take the shortcut through mean old Mr. Brown's yard. With a sister, I would never be lonely or afraid.

I don't remember exactly when my sister-lust began, but it was in full force by the time I was 6 years old. That was the year my mother had her fourth baby, and to my horrified indignation, it was a boy! She called me from the hospital with the "good" news, and I snapped, "That's not fair, I already have two brothers." This new one turned out to be Peter, and he was, and still is, a wonderful brother, but, alas, he was not a sister. That is when I began my search for a sister by holding open casting calls, conducting interviews, and auditioning unsuspecting prospects.

I searched for a sister in Mrs. Wright's kindergarten class. The girls tended to congregate around the tea set, but I could never navigate the tyranny of the doll corner, so I skipped around it instead. It is difficult to find a sister when the room is spinning. In those days, you had to be able to skip in order to pass kindergarten. Needless to say, after all my practice, I passed with flying colors. When all the neighborhood kids gathered after supper to play Fox and Hounds, I joined in the game, but I was secretly scouting for sister material. Since the boys were always the hounds and I was a fox charging to safety, there was little opportunity to conduct any potential sister interviews.

At last when I was in junior high, I won the double jackpot. At almost the same time, I became the proud sister of new baby Laura, and I found my very own best friend Denise. I was thrilled. Denise said we were even better than sisters. Being the proud owner of both an older and a younger sister, she knew about this. We did everything possible together. We did homework and went ice-skating. We practiced dancing and kissing while standing in front of a full-length mirror. We intended to be ready. We compared our flat chests daily, searching in vain for signs of progress. My sisterly love, unlike my breasts, grew daily. I was happy. Then, one sweltering summer afternoon, on Broadway outside the Community Theater, our mothers argued about whose turn it was to drive us home from the movies, and my mother exploded in that way she did so well. Mrs. A, Denise's mother, was horrified. Suddenly I was no longer welcome in Denise's home. This could never happen to real sisters, I thought sadly.

For a while we tried sneaking. I was pretty good at this, having been trained by necessity, but best friends require consistency and repetition and endless opportunities for gossip. It just didn't work. We faded out. In high school, Debbie replaced Denise, but that friendship lacked passion and obsession. And then, in my freshman year of high school, I lost my little sister when she died suddenly. It seemed that I did not have what it takes to be in the sacred sisterhood.

It wasn't until a few years later when I visited my new boyfriend at his home that my sister quest gained momentum. I was a shy college sophomore, and Lee was a French-speaking junior. Little did we know that our Woodstock transformation was lurking just around the corner. Decked out in a dainty, turquoise dress I sewed for the occasion, I was looking good. Lee met me at the train, and I nervously prepared myself to meet his parents. I don't remember the first interaction with my future in-laws, but I do remember walking into their house. I could tell right away something was different. I was in a foreign land, an unknown culture. There were bold paintings on the walls, fur rugs on the floor, orchids hanging from the ceiling, and food overflowing the fridge.

This was a house of abundance, drama, and beauty—a house of sisters!! Lee had forgotten to mention that he had three younger, adoring sisters. I was immediately surrounded. Peals of laughter and screeches of glee alternated with sobs of anguish and back again. I was dizzy with delight. The girls wanted to touch me, question me, and show me everything. They bombarded me with caresses I had never been given and questions I had never been asked. "Do you love our brother? Are you wearing a bra? Do you want me to do your makeup?" I was a teenager from a small town, raised in a house of brothers. We did not raise our voices except to cheer at baseball games. Passion was unacceptable. I couldn't believe that people actually emoted this way. I was charmed. I think Lee lost me utterly and won me undeniably that very day. My wish had come true in triplicate. I had found not one, but three sisters.

Thirty years later, I am still swept away by my sisters (in-law). We scream, gush, and gossip. I was in their lives as they transitioned through puberty and boyfriends into careers, husbands, and children. My participation was both ensured and relished. Recently the conversation has turned to menopause and college admissions. I can now almost keep up with the rapidly shifting emotions; I've had lessons from the best.

They taught me how to give good mushy hugs and make ear-splitting squeals of joy. I've learned about living with enthusiasm and appreciating beauty wherever it can be made or found. They helped me to be proud and competent and to love better. They support me when I am up or down, fascinating or boring. As you probably guessed, I did marry Lee. Please don't tell my husband this possibility: I may have married him because it was a package deal.

Goddess Salad Dressing Recipe

Those sisters of mine may not be quite other worldly or holy, but they are close enough to being Goddesses to remind me of the best salad dressing it is possible to make. This recipe is in honor of Jody, Jill, and Nancy. Thanks for having me!

I used to make this every week at the Golden temple in the 70's. In those days, I used a professional-size blender. It was easy then, and it still is.

Blend the following Ingredients:

- 1/2 cup tahini
- 1/3 cup apple cider or balsamic vinegar
- 1 tablespoon tamari (soy sauce)
- Juice of 1 lemon juice (lime juice will also work)
- 1-3 cloves garlic
- 1/3 cup water
- 2 tablespoon dried parsley
- 1 scallion
- 1 tablespoon honey
- 1/2 cup olive oil
- Fresh parsley and/or oregano if available

Take a taste and adjust if needed. Then pour the dressing into a jar and it will keep for at least a week in the refrigerator. Enjoy it on salad, sandwiches, or for dipping vegetables. You can even water it down and use it as a sauce over rice.

To Life!

Some words can only be whispered. This one, in particular, is rarely spoken in conversation. It is a political hot potato tossed about in every national election campaign. It is screamed back and forth at marches, sit-ins, and debates. There are few actual descriptions of it found in print. Even those people who support it in principle do not want to talk about it publicly. Yet many who are adamantly against it in public embrace it in private when the need arises. Few things encompass such paradoxes. The word I am hard-pressed to say is abortion.

As a woman who birthed four children, some already grown, I have been deeply immersed in the mothering enterprise for some time now. Between my own children, a couple of foster children, being a teacher and now a therapist, children have been my primary focus. From the depths of my heartfelt commitment to all children, from my passion for motherhood, from my reverence for God's creation, I must now speak the unspeakable and share my secret.

I remember that fateful morning when the little glass vial turned blue; I was pregnant. This time there was neither elation nor that sense of new worlds unfolding. There was only a sickening knot of dread. My thoughts kept traveling into dead-end corners: *Make it go away. Give me another chance. How can a teeny azure ring create such havoc? Maybe if I look again the blue circle will not be there, pointing up at me like a scolding finger.*

Lee and I wept. We began the long, agonizing process of decision-making. I was a mother who honored children and the sanctity of the family. I derived untold delight in my four very different children. I knew that we were linked by blood and destiny. So how could I even consider terminating this life just beginning in my womb?

I looked around for guidance. Where could I hear personal testimonials, attend a lecture, or read some books like *Five Women Who Had an Abortion and Went on to Great Things* or *How to Love Your Way Through An Abortion*? I needed a priest or a rabbi to place a reassuring arm on my shoulder and tell me that God would forgive me.

So how did we decide? A friend suggested that I listen to my heart. I tried to listen. Either my heart was not speaking or my hearing was seriously impaired. I heard, "A baby is a sacred trust, a gift from God." If I discarded this fetus like a used tissue, I would be destroying a life. I'd be reborn as a cockroach. (I can get pretty dramatic during a long sleepless night.)

My heart also said, "I do not want a baby. Four children are enough. I want to have time for my family, my husband, and myself. I want to begin the next phase of my life. I want to travel, to write, to volunteer more. I want to make a difference in the world. I want to laugh more, hug longer, and worry less."

Lee and I began to learn this lesson of shared pain. We have had disagreements. We have had losses. But this was different. We suffered this separately unable to come together. I was angry with him for doing this to me. I know we did it together; yet the anger remained. I was the one with life growing inside me. I was the one who felt nauseous every morning. I was the one who would have to endure labor and childbirth. He was angry at his helplessness. What could he do? What

106

could he say? We both knew that the final decision must rest with me. My body would bear the pregnancy and birth or the abortion and loss.

I wanted this decision to be lifted from me. *Just tell me God's will and I will do it.* Could someone put up a neon sign? I'm a little too dense for the subtle hints. God allowed this pregnancy, so it must have been God's will. But God also gave me free will and the access to a safe, accessible termination procedure. If there really is a God, she must be a loving entity who understands mistakes.

I know that abortion is *never* a good choice, but it is sometimes *the* choice. It was my choice this time. I chose life: the life of the four children who needed me, the life of my husband, pressured to provide for us, and the lives of others who I might change through my work. And my life. I chose my life. I was not sure that I had the physical strength and the inner forces to bring another being into the world.

Exactly who is it that controls a woman's conception, birth, or termination? A recent newspaper photo showed a dozen officials posing after signing into law a new abortion ban. They were all white, male, and well over 50. How is it that my body became theirs to shape?

Abortion has actually been part of life as far back as we know. Native Americans knew the herbs to use to terminate a pregnancy. Egyptians performed abortions. In India the secret methods are passed reverentially from midwife to midwife. Perhaps more highly evolved beings know how to prevent conception with thought control (I'm working on the technique, but obviously without much success).

Many ancient cultures explain that the soul does not enter the body until the fourth month. That moment when new mothers thrill to the first quickening movement within our wombs is actually the grand entrance of the child's soul. It thus follows that an abortion in the first trimester destroys a living organism but not a conscious, individual soul. That helped ease my mind a little.

Miscarriages, abortions, and stillbirths are not for public conversation. They still trail the dark miasma of back room, illicit operations, of failure and blame. Women's souls grow heavy with the memories. We women must speak of these secret things in order to banish the shame and sorrow we carry. We love to share baby birth stories. Perhaps it is time to share baby loss stories.

Two out of every three women have had an abortion and everyone, including all those silver-haired white lawmakers restricting Planned Parenthood and access to women's health care, has someone they care about who has had an abortion. I agree that life is precious, but I believe we need to take better care of the lives that are already here. Let's help AIDs orphans in Africa and children being trafficked. Did you know that in the United States 16.3 million children under 18 are hungry and malnourished? Why don't we hear public cries of outrage about them?

Now, alone in my room, I consider how old my unborn child would be if I kept her. Would she have my overlapping toes or my husband's luminous eyes? I cannot help but wonder. Do I regret my abortion? Well yes, of course I regret it. I will always carry this remorse as lovingly as a new baby. Would I make the same decision now? Maybe not, but I can and must live with that decision. I am doing the best I can in this journey of life. I have four vibrant children and a loving husband who still makes me laugh. I am a healthy woman attempting to live a righteous existence. I am all too aware of my shortcomings, I rarely forget my failings, and I live with the sadness of my past mistakes, but I am okay. That may not sound like much, but I think it's pretty damn impressive.

So here's to life!

Gandhi and Goldilocks

I was choking on the dust. The temperature was at least 40 degrees warmer than I am accustomed to and the constant jolts sent my stomach up into my throat. I was hungry, but afraid to eat, and thirsty but the warm water in the bottle rolling around at my feet held no appeal. It felt as if we had been traveling forever.

Out the window arid expanses of fields with desperate patches of scraggly corn, spotty cotton plants and miniature banana trees flashed by. You would be hard-pressed to find a postcard photo opportunity: beauty was not the common denominator here.

A barefoot girl stood drawing water from a well, a man in ragged robes squatted beside his tiny stand, a couple of dozen shriveled fist-sized oranges between his haunches; A group of half-naked children huddled outside a stick and waddle hut watched us drive by the village; cows were standing by the buildings, lying in the road, even inside the huts, with clearly outlined rib cages, they appeared to be skeletons. Colorfully wrapped women were working in the fields. These scenes flashed by our windows as we drove on.

My 9-year-old's singsong chant interrupted my reverie, and I remembered. We were in India. Lee and I, and our two younger children, Shanti and Avi, had made it to this land of stories, wonder, and enchantment. Via plane, train, and now jeep, we had left the congestion of New Delhi far behind. Moving through the dust with a purpose, we were on our way to Anand Niketan Ashram in Gujarat. Our invitation was from Harivallabh Parikh who lived and walked and was

110

jailed with Mahatma Gandhi 60 years ago! In our capacity as US Peace Secretary to Servas International we were invited to his ashram.

Three quarters of a century ago Gandhi sent Bhai-ji "respected brother" as he is known to thousands of villagers, to the most remote tribal area in one of the poorest states in India with little more instructions than, "go and work there, the people need you." He and his new bride arrived to a chilly reception from the Adivasis, the aboriginal people there. The couple camped under a tree until at last one kind-hearted man relented and took them into his home. Today Bhai-ji is beloved throughout India, as an international speaker and a relentless worker for peace and progress. Chosen last year by Week Magazine, India's *Time*, as Man of the Year, you might think that in his 70's he would be slowing down, enjoying his grandchildren and sleeping late. But then you have not met Bhai-ji!

The car detoured around a washed-out dip in the road, and my head banged against the roof as we turned in through a gateway. Our silent driver came to a stop, and I looked up at a blue sign on the white-washed gate: ANAND NIKETAN ASHRAM or ABODE OF JOY. This is a community built on Gandhian principles to establish a fellowship of brother (and sister) hood, peace and equality while working for economic development.

We breathed a big sigh of relief, unfolded our stiff legs, and tumbled out. The place appeared deserted. We stood with our bags in the courtyard. One thing you must learn to do in India, to avoid frustration and high blood pressure, is wait. Everything happens in its own time no matter what your personal agenda might be. This is often hard for Westerners but let me assure you, in a battle between your will and India's, the one with the weight of centuries will prevail. So we waited!

Finally to our amazement, we were greeted by a lovely young woman dressed in a half eastern and half western style. As soon as she opened her mouth, there was no mistaking; this was an American. Jennifer was a Servas intern working at the Ashram for the year.

After settling into our bare little dorm room, where the bathroom had a bucket and a hose for a shower, we returned downstairs to find the courtyard swarming with people. That evening was a holiday, and all the children lined up to receive a penny and a blessing from Bhai-ji. He was seated cross-legged on a wooden porch-swing dressed in the traditional saffron Khadi cloth. Each child walked up in matching frayed and faded lavender school uniforms, this year's bolt of fabric, kissed Bhai-ji's feet, and held out cupped hands to receive the penny. At the next day's festival, they would enjoy the sugar cane treat that their penny could buy.

We quickly settled into a routine. Avi was swept up in a tide of young boys. At each school recess, we heard cries of "Abi, Abi" calling him to join in the cricket game. Shanti was soon in a close relationship with three young European women as they shared travel stories late into the night. Lee was given a tour of the bio-gas generators in the neighboring villages and then worked with the tree planting crew.

The schoolteacher in me was bursting with curiosity, so I walked over to the school. The classrooms were bare cement rooms with two thin, straw mats quickly spread out for the teacher and me. I hoped to be able to watch a normal day at school, but as I settled myself into a cross-legged position, the entire atmosphere transformed. The children put on a show for my benefit. The clear voices of little girls joined together. From their dramatic gestures, I surmised that they were singing about washing, planting, and harvesting. Drums begin to pound the beat as the boys marched around the room. Then with great dignity, the adolescent girls glided up to the front and sang a song scolding the boys for drinking and the girls for using too much makeup. I, in turn, taught them "Head, Shoulders, Knees and Toes" and "We Shall Overcome" while trying to keep my tears in check as they all joined with me in song.

Bhai-ji stays appraised of all the decisions and events occurring in his community and the large area of surrounding villages under his benign rule. He oversees the development of 1,100 Adivasi villages, totaling 1.5 million people often from his place of honor on the swing. We joined him, and he regaled us with stories. At fourteen, he ran away from his wealthy parents and joined the radical young Ganhdi-ji. He spun cloth with Gandhi, organized with him, and even went to jail with him. When he first arrived here after India's independence, which was closely followed by Gandhi's assassination, the land was covered in dense forests. The rajah would periodically arrive with his entire retinue, set up plush tents, and hunt tigers.

Eventually Harivallabh began to settle disputes in the villages. Sometimes he marked a spot equal in distance from the disputants' homes, where they could meet without loss of prestige. He would settle the disputes in a way both sides could accept. A man who killed a neighbor agreed to support the dead man's family. It was from these beginnings that the People's Court grew. It continues to meet twice a month under the spreading banyan tree and has been recognized nationally.

He explained to us the seemingly simple philosophy that guided his life, "Service to people is service to God," he says, "But the heart of the program is still the People's Court." He ends every session of People's Court by passing out sugar cane to all the children, "Because" he tells us, "justice should always be sweet!"

On our last night, there was a community gathering in our honor. We wished we had something to give or present. This was one of those moments like when Judy Garland and Mickey Rooney turn to each other and say, "I've got an idea. Let's put on a show!" And that was what we decided to do. We quickly settled on "Goldilocks and the Three Bears": it is short, has only a few roles, and offers opportunity for a little slapstick. The only problem is its focus on the blondeness of its main character—a minor point we choose to ignore.

After an afternoon of mask making and rehearsal, we were ready for the stage. "Once upon a time, there were three bears: a papa bear, a mama bear, and a little baby bear." The entire community turned out, and somehow, Bhai-ji translated as we performed. We will never know what he actually said, but the audience roared with laughter when Shanti broke the imaginary chair! It was a perfect end to our stay.

The next morning, we were on our way to Dharamsala in the mountains of northern India for an audience with the Dalai Lama. But that is another story.

114

A Sacred Ceremony

Choking sobs assault me from all directions. The air feels dense; shapes are only dimly perceivable. I am standing in the center of a dark basement, surrounded on all sides by weeping teenagers. They are sitting two and three deep against pillows, huddled on laps, perched on tables, and leaning against walls and knees. And still more keep arriving, walking down the stairs in twos and threes. They have rings in their noses and lips, shaved heads, jewelry made of screws, nuts, and bolts, and tattoos in strange places. Their clothes are ripped, ragged, and layered. Hair runs the gamut from purple to orange to green and combinations thereof. Today they are all hurting.

It is 5 PM on a Monday evening in March. Most of these young people stood up and walked out of school early today. My husband Lee and I are in the center of this crowded basement that is filled with expectant silences and charged emotions. There is a sense of danger, of desperation. Why are we here? What could possibly connect this group?

All of these young people are friends or acquaintances of Tommy—a cheerful, shy, skate-boarding 16-year-old boy. Three days ago, at dawn, he stood at the school flagpole and shot himself in the head.

Today is his funeral. These friends and schoolmates are forbidden to attend that funeral. The family, for complicated reasons of shame and fear, will not allow them in. The school will not even acknowledge the death for fear of copycat suicides. The message the kids are being given is "forget about the whole thing."

115

But that is, of course, not possible. They must find some way to acknowledge what happened and grieve before they can move on.

Everyone in the room has been touched in some way by this boy and by his (and our) senseless tragedy. They have been reeling all weekend with disbelief, horror, anger, and loss. Where do they put these feelings? How do they make sense of this tragedy? Can they choose to go on? What about those who have themselves considered suicide during long nights past and are afraid? Where are the adults willing to talk about life and death?

It seems to be up to us. Everyone in this room is looking to us. What can we possibly hope to offer? How can we ease the pain, comfort the mourning, and reassure these many pairs of eyes now turned beseechingly in our direction?

The basement is in the home of Rob, a middle-aged, unemployed, scraggly artist. He saw the rebellious youths of the town gathered day after day on a local street corner near his home and invited them to gather and organize at his house. One day our 15-year-old daughter informed me about a meeting at the home of this older man. *Hmm, this sounds a little strange.* I reacted with suspicion. So I gave him a call. "What's this I hear about meetings at your house (and who are you anyway)?'" Before we finished the conversation, I had offered to help. Pretty soon, he had a regular group of fifteen or twenty misfit kids meeting twice a week. I brought food, guest speakers, and a listening ear.

This continued in a quiet way for a couple of months. I enjoyed the ragtag group of rebels and lost souls. I appreciated that they, too, were on a quest for answers, for truth, for purpose; though they didn't exactly know it. Then this suicide happened. With nowhere else to go, knowing instinctively that they could not be alone, the students left school and headed to the dark but familiar basement. They brought friends. This began early Friday morning after word of the death spread throughout the school. School officials allowed the students to go to the guidance office, but they offered little comfort and no discussion or symbolic words.

Unable to tolerate silence in the face of this soul-shaking event, the students began to leave the school in small, silent streams. They gathered in Rob's basement... and others followed. But on Monday, incensed by the school's refusal to even mark the boy's passing with a moment of silence, and their exclusion from the funeral, they cut class and headed to The Basement. By noon the numbers were growing. I received the call from Rob, "What should we do?" After a quick consultation, Lee and I announced that we would be there at 5 PM to conduct a ceremony. There was no formal way to announce this: word simply spread.

Often it seems adults get frustrated with teenagers. They think the kids are causing way too much trouble with their laziness, sex, drinking, and drugs. Parents sometimes refer to this time as the long, dark tunnel. Witness the jokes and rolled eyes at the mention of teenagers. Some of us even cross the street to avoid them. Many would prefer to lock all 13-year-olds in a distant warehouse and let them out at 18 or 19. What a wonderful world it would be.

But would it really? What would a place without teenagers look like? It might at first seem peaceful, but it would soon become boring and lifeless. The world

117

would lack the yeast to get our creative bread to rise. Teens reflect the worst of us, the darkest recesses, the narcissism, the decadence; yet they hint at the best. They see through the falseness that we adults erect as protection. Those of us who are or have been parents, teachers, counselors, friends, or relatives of teenagers— and that includes just about all of us—must try to gain some perspective. Adolescents are the ones who force us to re-examine our ideals and prod us to step up and do what is right.

Our children's' sudden growth at adolescence is an outer metaphor of the powerful changes manifesting inwardly. The body is growing and changing, the mind is stretching, and the values and individual truths are trying to keep up. Adolescents are shaping their identities. No wonder this sometimes involves rejecting the family. They are searching for Truth. No wonder they are sometimes angry. They want the world to be Just. They are looking for signs of Hope. No wonder they are sometimes discouraged. They think about death because they are evaluating life. Why was I born? What is the purpose of my life? Do I want to live? But life can seem to be filled with struggle. This is where we can be ready to step in and say, "Yes. It is hard, but take my hand, and we will walk together."

So here we are, with little time to prepare, or consult each other, and no professional back up. As we are about to begin, the school administrator calls and asks if we would please have these kids back to normal so they do not play hooky tomorrow. The reporters from the local newspapers are elbowing their way in, and a few parents, looking bewildered and concerned, stand around in the doorways.

We begin by taking a deep breath. We set some ground rules. "Safety is a priority," we tell them. "We are here to support each other. When one person is speaking, everyone else is listening." Lee says a few words of opening and prayer and speaks about what happened. I sing a Native American song:

> *Ancient Mother, I hear you calling*
> *Ancient Mother, I hear your song*
> *Ancient Mother, I hear your laughter*
> *Ancient Mother, I taste your tears*

It is a mournful, haunting melody. As the echoing notes die away, the room is left in absolute, unbroken silence. Not a cough or a shuffle mars the still, almost holy silence.

We set the main candle on a small table and say, 'This candle is Tommy. We ask you to come up, one at a time, light your candle from the main one, and say a few words about Tommy, or how you are feeling, or simply stand in silence." Rob, as their spokesman and trusted adult, lights Tommy's candle and speaks first.

I am wondering if they will come up? What if no one responds? What if this pushes another child over the edge? What if this is too dangerous? All these doubts are rumbling around in me even as the procession begins. In respectful order and stillness, they step forward.

T. was so much fun.
You left us too soon. Why'd you do it?
I love you, man.
You were so beautiful. I miss you.
I didn't really know you but I wish I did.
Man, I know what you were thinking.
I'm so scared.

You could have asked us for help.

I won't forget you, buddy; you were my friend.

The room grows brighter with each candle lit and with each tear shed. Tommy's girlfriend, who first heard the news of his death over the loudspeaker at school, comes up to speak and collapses into paroxysms of hysterical sobbing. She is held and rocked and stroked by others as they return her to her place. There is an amoeba-like quality to this group, as if they are a single organism that gently thrusts out one unit from time to time and then gratefully receives it back into the whole. A few people come up and simply light a candle and stand in silence before being swallowed back by the group life force.

I look around the room: everyone is holding a candle. The dark room is glowing brightly but the despair is pulsating, pounding. What is the force we have unleashed? Do we know what we are doing? Can we keep these young, wounded souls from drowning in it? Can we turn the pain into healing?

Lee steps forward and asks everyone to look at the light all around them. 'This is your light. You have created it together. It is Tommy's gift to you. Please blow out your candle, but allow that light to penetrate through to your hearts. When you are feeling overwhelmed and hopeless think of that light and remember that you're not alone. Tommy's death will not be in vain because it has brought us together; it has given us a family where we can belong. I want everyone to stand up. Now reach out and be sure you are in contact with at least one other person. We have each other. We are not alone. We have formed a community.

And then we begin to sing. The words, the notes swell as our voices are joined by 100 more:

Amazing grace, how sweet the sound
That saved a soul like me
I once was lost, but now am found
Was blind but now I see

It is so important at this time in life that each young person feels a connection (through a person, a God, a sport, an animal, a cause) to the world. She must believe that there is meaning in the struggle, that she personally can make a difference, that she matters. And she needs to belong to something: a family, a community, a country, or a cause. I have had young people say to me, "I wish I had something to believe in." As a good mother, I would never let my child go without a meal. God forbid she should be hungry or wanting. Yet here are teenagers all around me who are starving for spiritual nourishment. How have we failed them? In old cultures, the youth were given a vision quest, a rite of passage that was guided by the elders. Today just living as a teenager is often a rite of passage. The challenges and terrors are there, but the guidance of a wise uncle/aunt, grandparent, midwife, or shaman is often missing.

Some adults can take our place in the community as guides for these young people. If we reach back to the strength and wisdom of our elders in the past and shape what we find to the needs of today, we will find the way to do the right thing. We are aiming for mighty transformation. We're on our way to the unknowable future and some of these rowdy, pierced teenagers will soon be the ones to lead the way. Imagine that! My only advice: Stay open, laugh a lot, and pray when possible. Hold hands. Here we go!

At last, there in the underground crypt, we blow out Tommy's candle. It has been snuffed out in the world and now here in this basement. We are in total darkness. The silence is broken only by a few sobs and an occasional sniffle. Silence.

There has been a shift here in this airless basement space. A group of random teenagers have come together and changed. Yes, they are scarred and will never be as innocent again. But they have grown. There is a dignity, a pride in their mourning. Some will grow stronger, kinder, and more compassionate. They will help each other to move forward. They will be heard. They will choose life, with its bumps and hard edges and injustices, but LIFE all the same. That, in the end, is Tommy's true gift to us.

*Clockwise Top Left: Moses
And Rami. Kiara and me.
Ashram in India 1992. Moses 1991.*

Top: My first-grade class photo at 62 York Avenue, 1956. I'm the one with pigtails on the right end of the middle row! Bottom: Teaching First Grade at 62 York Ave, 1987

LEAVES

My Modern Maturity

This year, despite my optimistic outlook, I collided with middle age. I wish I could report that I arrived with dignity and grace, but no, I was dragged there kicking and screaming. I did not go quiet into the evening song of menopause.

Let me assure you, I eat well: cancer-preventive greens, free-radical fruits, keep-it-moving roughage, and bone-firming tofu. I take daily vitamin supplements. Of course, I exercise, dragging myself to the gym with consistent irregularity, though I no longer imagine keeping pace with the Lycra-covered, toned woman on the next step machine. That washboard stomach does not enter even my wildest fantasies. My sights, in addition to my breasts, seem to have dropped. We are talking basic maintenance here. Success is now defined as simply slowing the inevitable decline.

Have you noticed how, in the last decade or so, we baby boomers have been surreptitiously redefining middle age? I can dress like a teenager, color away the gray, retinal-A the wrinkles, and liposuction the puckered rolls. I can have a baby at 45 and still try to decide what I want to be when I grow up. Menopause has entered the lexicon as a status symbol—sort of like that silver Porsche on my wish list. It sneaks up on you just when you stop thinking of training wheels and soccer games and start focusing on IRA's and nursing homes for aging parents. It has taken up undisputed residence when you find yourself examining you skin for melanomas rather than hickeys and when hot flashes become more familiar than arousal.

At 50, who am I kidding? Middle is only the polite word for it. I have already passed that Rubicon. I have probably lived more of my life than I have left to live. There are more memories than dreams in my future. No matter how upbeat we pretend to be, loss lies in wait for us. No more babies, no more innocence, no more appreciative whistles as we walk down the streets. Let's face it—this ride is picking up speed. The final destination is mortality, and death sits waiting on the road ahead. My particular cosmic kick in the seat of my pants was comprised of three distinct cataclysmic events:

One: After 25 years of interacting through our four children, Lee and I are about to be *home alone* for two weeks: just the two of us here with no kids. We have hardly spent time together without children. But now, our two children still living at home are going to Hawaii with their aunt. What will it be like for us? What will we do? We might have uninterrupted conversation or maybe silence. We can eat anytime or not at all. Visions of sex in the afternoon on the kitchen counter fill my unleashed fantasies. Then what? I detect a pattern here: two weeks this year, the entire summer next year. The nest is beginning to look practically vacant.

Two: I waved goodbye to my youngest offspring, squared my shoulders and gritted my teeth as I turned to do battle with the empty-nest demons. Just then I received a call from Son No. 1. "Mom, we have something important to tell you." My mind began to race. I imagined the worst—he was arrested again, he's moving to join the Zapatista's revolution, and he never wants to see his sell-out parents again. "Kim and I are expecting a baby." I quietly hand the phone to my husband, but my head is exploding with screams. *Oh my God! A baby!* Does this mean that I am going to be a grandmother? Me? I have not yet decided that I am finished *having* babies. *Yikes! Okay. Breathe.* I can do this. This is a Hallmark moment. This is great news, right?

Three: The third punch, the knockout, came before my breath returned to normal, before I have even confessed my approaching grandmother status publicly. Our younger daughter—a high school senior honors student, striking beauty and confident, wise soul—announced her love for a man who is closer to my age than hers and her teacher besides. They are, so she said, deeply in love and intend to leave after graduation and live off the land in some distant northern homestead. No college, no travel, no carefree development for her. It will be starvation, pregnancy, unrelenting cold, and barefoot destitution. I didn't know that people still do that living-off-the-land thing. Nobody wants to live without electricity, let alone computers, these days! Perhaps if I reasoned with her, argued, and demanded, it would all go away. I considered standing guard at her door with a chastity belt ready or locking her in her room until she gave up the plan. Maybe if I ignored it, this, too, would pass. On the other hand, begging might be my only hope. I raised a stubborn, young woman. Changing her mind will not be easy.

You know what surprises me most as I cycle through the stages of life? How I, a bona fide child of the '60s, ended up sounding like my parents? I was going to do it all naturally, employing the wisdom of the Buddha's non-attachment. I knew about reincarnation before it was a 900 number. I had the irreverence of

Richard Pryor, the faith of Martin Luther King, Jr, and the cynicism of Watergate. My eyes were wide open. I knew where I was going. Now, suddenly, I was not so sure.

There is nobility in accepting the inevitable with grace. I told myself to picture this: a clean house, a glass of wine, a worthy book in hand, and my good-looking partner nearby. Hmmm, so far, so good. Add in a grandchild to take to the park now and then before returning her to her parents who get to deal with the tantrums, learning disabilities, and body piercings. As for my homesteading daughter: give me a pair of work boots and a hoe, I'm heading west for the spring planting. But just for a visit. Then I'll return home where I can turn up the thermostat, run the dishwasher, and order take-out sushi. So this is middle age? Maybe I can get used to it. Let's call it *prime of life* instead.

Touched by Angels

Hope is the thing with feathers
that perches in the soul –
And sings the tune without the words—
And never stops – at all –
                    Emily Dickinson

Have you ever heard that the threshold between this world and the next occasionally thins allowing us to peek through to the other side? Some describe a tunnel of light after a near-death experience; others relate dream visions or meditation insights. Well, it happened for me on a Sunday evening just before sunset. The weekend was winding down from its normal frenzy of activity. My family was quietly reading on the living room couch, the picture of domestic contentment.

Suddenly a shadow darkened the large window across from us, and before we knew it, the window exploded in slow motion into a million diamond-like crystals. I am not sure the exact order of what happened next, but I know that everyone was in motion. My husband threw himself protectively across my daughter's head, pressing her into the couch. I sat momentarily stunned before running barefoot across what we later saw was a ten-foot swathe of shattered glass. In the kitchen, I found a large creature churning the air with its five-foot wingspan. Dishes, African violets, and food hurled in all directions, as the wild creature strained against the kitchen window. It was a male turkey complete with neck wattles and heel spurs. Having entered our house with stunning determination, he was now surprisingly anxious to depart. It took some maneuvering, but I managed to remove the screen and hold him back with it while I opened the window and watched him fly free, apparently unhurt. We were left behind in the ensuing stillness, stunned and shaken, to clean up the damage.

The Irish say that a wild bird in the house portends a death. I don't know, but after two nights of wild turkey dreams, our friends' 10-year-old daughter died, killed instantly in a morning car crash. Later that day at their home, I stood watch before little Emma as she lay in the room where she was born 10 years ago. Today her parents brought her home from the Emergency Room determined to prepare and bury her themselves on their property. Except for a bandaged head, her young body looked perfect. The angels must have been drawing near. If only I could have turned down my own internal humming, I might have been able to hear them. *Hummm. I have to call the plumber, get the groceries, pick up my son. Hummm. I'm scared, hungry, tired. Hummm. What do I say to Emma, to her parents, to God?* At last, I grew quiet. Emma's young cousin sat by the bedside reading stories to her. I asked, "Which story is Emma's favorite?" She was quick to answer, "'The Lion and the Mouse'."

Was that the brush of wings against my shoulder as I removed the hospital gown from Emma's cold form? Her mother asked me to dress her in her own clothes rather than the hospital gown. I pulled yesterday's turquoise baseball jersey over her head. Ever so gently, I rubbed my thumb across her little cuts and bruises from days past, wanting them to hurt her again. She hit her first home run last night and, though normally a quiet child, she pranced with glee. Could she have known that it was her last night on earth?

131

In the evening, I remembered the wild turkey as we women gathered to sit vigil with Emma through the dark hours, talking quietly, crying, and knitting socks for her cold feet. Heaven seemed to touch down in the barn where the men worked through the night sawing, sanding, and polishing. At last her little coffin was lined with embossed silk brought from Japan by her Grandpa after World War II.

I woke to what might have been the whir of many wings in the early morning. I shook myself awake as the sounds merged into a delegation of lawn mowers manned by a teenage crew. Emma's big brother directed at least a dozen high school students who prepared the grounds for the funeral ceremony. Hundreds of people, including Emma's entire 4th-grade class, arrived in the afternoon to speak and sing, laugh, and cry, as they remembered one little girl.

Ten years is not a long time. Emma didn't have enough time to grow up; she was just getting started. The writer Chaim Potok says that human beings live less than the time it takes to blink an eye. He reminds us that we are each responsible to fill our tiny span of life with meaning. Emma's life was brief, yet her impact was immeasurable. Those of us left behind were sad, even angry, but we all sensed a glimpse of that threshold when Emma's horse, saddle glaringly empty, led the procession to her graveside. Few were dry-eyed when the young driver of the truck that swerved into a small Toyota, crushing a little girl in the back seat, was welcomed by the bereaved family. Forgiveness was the only option considered. Right before our eyes, transformation slipped through the clouds and touched us. I heard families talking about life and death. I saw community members greet each other and forgive old offenses now united by tears. Most of us held our children to us as if being spared this time.

Maybe it was a sense of deep knowing or simply a reordering of priorities. Whatever it was, it stayed with me throughout the following weeks. What really mattered? Was I wasting too much time worrying? Was I loving my children and cherishing my husband enough? Could I choose happiness right now before it is too late?

In some Native American traditions, the wild turkey is the giveaway bird. In the traditional giveaway ceremony, people offer their worldly possessions to others as a way to simplify their life, practice generosity, and remember their priorities once again. That turkey was calling to me.

I could feel the threshold closing as my fears and resentments descended once more into their well-worn place between my shoulder blades. I was distracted by the symphonies of to-do lists enumerated in indelible pen. I stopped crying. I sang less. I forgot to look up at the sky. But one morning, a week later, I found a small fluttering feather behind the dish drain. It was golden brown edged in white. I stopped what I was doing and stood still. I listened for the sound of wings. Then I taped it to the wall so that I cannot, I will not, forget.

Pizza Pile-Up Recipe

I bet you know this feeling; it has been a long day and an even longer week. Maybe you have even accomplished some good work. Regardless, your reserves are depleted and you are ready to relax. For us, this day is usually Thursday. The weekend is near, but making dinner??? That is just not going to happen.

This is when we need Pizza Power to the rescue! It is our go-to twice-a-month meal when we just don't have it in us to get creative or energetic with dinner. The meal is usually good for a second day or becomes a good lunch.

Here's how it works. We order a basic cheese pizza from our local parlor. We pick it up as we are leaving the gym and heading home. Once home, we snap into action.

Anything in the vegetable drawer is fair game— ideally broccoli, zucchini, mushrooms and a green, like spinach, chard, kale, or some mix thereof. Grab an onion and a clove of garlic and slice, dice, and chop. Throw everything in the frying pan: onion first, then mushroom and garlic, add the broccoli, sauté for a few more minutes, then add a tiny bit of water and quickly cover. Let it steam for a minute before adding the zucchini and the greens and cook for another minute. Not too much. You want the vegetables to be cooked but not soggy. Several minutes later, your vegetables are done.

Meanwhile you can throw together a salad, heat the pizza, and then pile the vegetables on board. And I mean really heap them onto that slice. It turns out that we are eating vegetables that are held in place by a thin carrier of pizza; more veggie than crust! Lee adds red pepper flakes; I add nutritional yeast. Either way, we happily end our Thursday evening satiated, without cancelling out our efforts at the gym.

Because of this recipe, it has become almost painful for my family to eat pizza straight from the shop. They just never put enough veggies on it!

Possible Ingredients:

- 1 onion, chopped
- 2 cloves garlic (optional)
- 8 mushrooms, sliced
- 1 head of broccoli, cut into bite size
- 1 zucchini, sliced
- 1 cup of spinach
- 1 teaspoon olive oil
- Salt to taste
- Red pepper (optional)

Place as much of the cooked vegetables as you can get onto a warm slice of pizza and enjoy.

Bedtime Lullaby

In *Fiddler on the Roof,* Tevya turns to his wife and asks her, "Do you love me?" "Do I love you?" is her amazed response. "For twenty-five years my bed is his. If that's not love, what is?" I may agree with her, but after 25 years, my husband and I have had love but no bed to share.

You probably think that it is obvious: married couples, here in the US of A, sleep in beds. "Of course," you might remark, "Where else, the bureau drawer?" When people need a bed, most go out and buy one. I have heard that it is done all the time. For us, it was not so simple.

Let me tell you the odyssey of my nuptial bed. It started around the time of our anniversary. Lee and I do not normally make all that much out of these occasions, but somehow this one seemed significant. We had been through a lot together: 300 months as a married couple, four children, and 12,000 meals across the table (I counted). We were doing okay; sometimes we even liked each other. Then came this strange notion that I wanted a bed, a real bed, not simply a mattress on the floor. I'm not sure why. Perhaps I was ready to say goodbye to the '60s. Lord knows it was about time. Maybe I was tired of everyone tromping across my holy matrimonial altar, or perhaps it was becoming too monumental a task to raise myself from the horizontal to the vertical on short notice. Whatever the reason, I wanted a bed.

For years I had witnessed *bed evidence* in other couples' homes. Like WMD inspectors in Iraq, I was on the search. Excusing myself to go to the bathroom, I'd make a quick detour. There it would be: their master bedroom with a large bed perched arrogantly center stage. Did they find it on Craig's List: *Queen-sized bedroom set, good condition*? Or were they enticed by those colorful Sunday add supplements that show a perfect bedroom set complete with curtains? Why was it that something that appeared to be possible, even easy, for so many became a major event of deep meaning and insurmountable challenge for me?

I lobbied, knowing what worked best when dealing with a complacent husband. It always helped to ease ultimatums into the conversations during appropriate lulls.

"Did you see what happened to the Israeli settlers on the West Bank?"

"Hmmm."

"It's time we had a bed."

Once I stood directly in front of the TV during the Super Bowl, "How about we get a bed?"

After a number of these subtle hints, I finally had his attention. Never underestimate the value of simple erosion. Then again "Don't even think of touching me until we are in our own bed" also works. He surrendered.

On a bright June day, when new brides blossom, we were off to the bed store. You know, it's kind of sexy to shop for a bed. You try out these different styles and picture the illicit acts that might occur. As I sprawled supine across one bed after another, my sluggish imagination began to kick in. This one is tall and austere, perfect to have him come begging. Another with posts would work great for that bondage scene. Then there's the Oriental; do it backwards and upside down variety. I don't know the details of Lee's fantasies, but the retorts were flying, our temperatures rising, the salesman blushing. The result: our check was written, and we became proud owners of a brand new bed!

Alas, upon paying, we discovered that the bed was not yet built. The owner assured us we would have our bed by August. Two more months! After all this time, you might think, what's the rush? Well, I really wanted my bed immediately, not two months down the road.

In early August, we got the long-awaited phone call. "The bed is here. Come and get it." You mean to say we had to pick it up; they didn't deliver? There was no way that bed would fit into our Subaru. But many tense hours later, after roping our brand new bed precariously to the roof, we were home. *O boy, O boy, I couldn't wait to sleep on that beautiful bed tonight.*

Wait a minute. There was a catch. I should have known. Of course, we couldn't get the headboard or the footboard up the narrow staircase of our old house. Maneuvering this way and that, cursing each other, scratching it, we finally gave up. Destiny appeared to be playing a role. I was sure that the universe did not want us to have a bed. Why? Would it bring bad luck? *Return it,* I thought. *Sell it. Buy a different house. Saw the headboard in two.* Yes, we thought of everything, but at last we remembered that God helps those who help themselves. *It just might fit in through our daughter's upstairs bedroom window.*

It took three more weeks before we had a free day. Peering at the window opening, extension ladder stretching skywards, I handed Lee the footboard, and he climbed up the trembling ladder with our cherry masterpiece tucked adorably under one arm. With a last look over my shoulder and a whispered prayer to the protective saint of conjugal bliss, I raced around the corner, into the house, and up the stairs just in time to grab the bed as it came through the window. Hallelujah! But if we had learned anything in our elder wisdom, it was not to celebrate too soon. The headboard was considerably larger.

Fast forward a sweaty hour and try not to imagine the explicatives or the interpersonal wounds reopened. We managed to get the bed in and assembled. The rolled-up rug that had waited for months was smoothed on the floor. All was looking good.

Not so fast! There were only three thin slats on the bed frame, enough to support a box spring, but we did not own a box spring. Lee raced to the lumber store to buy some plywood. They were closed. That night, bed towering above us, we slept pressed into the corner of our now forlorn mattress on the floor watching bed shadows flicker mockingly over our heads.

It may now be clear that certain things do not come easily for us, but we persevered. No obstacle is too great for our resilient determination. The next day, the plywood was cut and placed. The mattress settled comfortably into its new quarters. The room was clean, and the pillow shams and quilt were practically glowing with *Better Homes and Garden* luster.

"It looks like a magazine picture," my daughter gushed. "You need a beautiful nightgown to go with it."

Not only did I have no negligee worthy of this bed, but I was grimy, tired, and it was that time of the month. Besides, my husband and I weren't even speaking. I slept on the couch that night. Perhaps I'd be ready for a grown-up bed soon.

Kilimanjaro

Surely there can be few more dramatic ways to welcome in the New Year than on the majestic slopes of Mt. Kilimanjaro in Tanzania, Africa. Lee's dream of climbing the highest freestanding peak in the world for our 25th anniversary was about to come true. My personal fantasy involved piña coladas on the beach, but that, alas, was not to be.

Our first close glimpse of the mountain came at the Amboseli campground when we were on safari. Shortly after setting up flimsy tents in the middle of elephant territory, we gazed skyward; the clouds had dispersed, and there was Mt. Kilimanjaro towering above us, snow-capped and daunting. Lee assured us that this was the north peak and that we were climbing the south, which was much friendlier (yeah, right)!

Day 1: On January 1st, Lee, Shanti (15), Avi (almost 10), and I prepared ourselves to begin the ascent. Gear packed and ready, bodies conditioned, spirits willing, we woke up in Marangu as ready as we'd ever be and headed to the gate with our friends and travel companions Gretchen, Poppy, and Pat from Boston. There we met our nine porters, two cooks, and Zawadi, our mountain guide. Shouldering daypacks, we hiked through the steamy rainforest accompanied by the hot sun, the red dust (African snow), and baboon serenades. Zawadi carried a huge boombox on his shoulder, reggae music filling the sky. Soon we crossed a narrow, crude bridge. It was as if a line was drawn on the earth; the change from jungle to more familiar forest terrain was so abrupt. By early afternoon, we reached our day's destination—the Mandara huts—

where we were served popcorn and tea. After dinner, Lee performed his evening ritual of purifying water for the next day before we settled into our bunks. There was no turning back now.

Day 2: Twice as long. Each twist and turn on the trail opened new panoramic vistas. The birds sang, and Zawadi claimed there were lions in residence who must have heard us coming. "Pole-pole" was an oft-repeated phrase. It was the Swahili mountain mantra for "slowly, slowly." They say it is the only way to make it to the top and we heard it called out all day.

We arrived at Horumbo after trudging our way through spectacular alpine meadows and a dense forest. Horumbo looks like a bustling miners' camp. Stark scrabble ground and precariously tilting cook shacks were marked by the thin trail of rising blue smoke. A ring of metal-roofed A-frame bunkhouses, one latrine shack with cold water, and a dining room lined with picnic tables completed this encampment. We found a scurrying mix of nationalities: German, French, Japanese, Norwegian, and a few American hikers. The tourists could be distinguished by their mostly white skin color and bright, shiny mountain gear. Then there were dozens of African porters: dark skin, bright eyes, and jambo greetings. They wore sandals, loafers, and a hodgepodge of winter clothing that had been collected by various means. Unlike the Sherpas of Nepal, these men are unfamiliar with the ice and snow since the only cold weather in Tanzania is at the top of Mt. Kilimanjaro.

While there, Avi invented a card game called Horumbo. Shanti was welcomed into the cook hut and helped with dinner prep. By the time our dinner of cabbage and potatoes was eaten, the sky was overflowing with stars we could practically reach up and grab, and it was cold enough to send us diving into our sleeping bags.

Day 3: We had an early start. The day's hike would take us from 12,000 to 15,500 feet. Our hearts, lungs, and legs were feeling the altitude. Our pace was slow but steady, and we managed some singing, conversation, and plant identification, but mostly we trudged in silence. The rhododendrons we had seen in the morning were proud, stately trees, but by afternoon, they have become shrubs no taller than ten inches. Everything was struggling for survival—a scary thought. Then we came to an ominous crossing: the last water on the mountain. We had entered an alpine desert. From that moment on, we had only the water we carried with us and one liter each that the porters carried. *Pole-pole.* We walked, rested, walked, talked, groaned, walked, laughed, collapsed, and walked some more.

The porters called Avi "power boy." They were not used to seeing children climb this far. Our quiet pace was shattered as we scattered to let two porters race by us, guiding a one-wheeled stretcher down the mountain. We caught a glimpse of a woman strapped in. Gulp. Could that be one of us tomorrow? There was no oxygen carried on this mountain. The only way to cure altitude sickness—which can be fatal—is to get down to a lower level, fast.

At last we saw a Kibu hut ahead. Our stopping place for the night. And we thought Horumbo was bare bones! This looked like the end of the world. There was no plant or animal life, no water, just a cement bunker and ten bunks in each of two bare, cold rooms. We collapsed into deep unconsciousness until we were awakened for a meager soup dinner. Most people were unable to eat due to nausea caused by the altitude. The mood was somber as we pulled out and sorted all the layers we had packed: silk, polypropylene, wool, fleece, Gore-Tex, hats, scarves, mittens, headlamps, and carefully hoarded snacks of Tiger's Milk bars, Skittles, and, of course, water. There was nothing more to be done. We were asleep by 8:30 PM.

Day 4: Wake up call was three hours later at 11:30 PM. One large Frenchman in our room was loudly groaning in his bunk, overtaken by altitude sickness. Nine shadowy shapes silently dressed before emerging for tea. At that point, reality had become dim and dreamlike. By 12:30 AM, we were suited up and on our way. We set off single file in the dark, following the only thing you could see—the feet in front of your own. Our line of twinkling headlamps began the eight-hour ascent to the top. But after fifteen minutes of this awkward dance, Shanti, ever the practical one, said, "This is no fun," and returned to the bunkhouse. Zawati led her back and then reappeared. A few minutes later, Avi saw the wisdom in Shanti's plan and begged to return too. When Zawati came back, he was, for the first time in his mountain experience, suffering from altitude sickness. It probably had something to do with the rapid ups and downs of bringing our kids back to camp. There was nothing for him to do but return to the bunk as well. Without Zawati, we came under the care of a young man in a tight pink parka who had never led an expedition. But his inexperience was not something we could think about. The path was a steep, hard-scrabble, lunar surface. There was neither plant nor animal life, only strange, subhuman creatures shuffling agonizingly along.

144

Above and below, we saw the blinking line of barely moving headlamps winding up and down the zigzagging path and heard retching as we shuffled along, a procession of octogenarian-like humans. One step, two steps. Pant, pant. We leaned on walking sticks and waited for our hearts to stop racing. I tried not to think of the pain and wondered why I decided to do this to myself and pay for it besides! *Om Mane Padme Om*—each of my words was a step. *Don't think and don't look up.* Time disappeared; there was only the next step. If we stopped, the chill seeped into our bones. The water bottles in our pack were turning to ice. *Om Mane Padme Om.* After four hours, the upside down crescent moon rose orange over a peak behind us. When I was not too dizzy, I looked back to the moon to give me courage. *Almost there,* it assured me. Finally, we noticed the hint of light just beginning to keep its promise. There would be a morning! As we made our final steps to the peak, the sun exploded over the horizon, illuminating a landscape of cloud-mountains. We made it! 19,500 feet, the rooftop of Africa, four miles up towards heaven.

I will spare you the trip down and the two days of crippled hobbling that followed. Suffice it to say that I will wait another 25 years before I do that again. I am sure Lee is already hatching plans for the next expedition, so feel free to submit your suggestions.

Rain, Rain Go Away

If you know what's good for you, you'll go away, right now. Just go. Stop reading this. I can feel a rant coming on. I'm sorry, but I can't seem to help it. Walk away now and be spared. Consider yourself warned. Are you still here? I believe in the power of positivity and the laws of attraction and good karma and all that sweet stuff, but sometimes the reptilian brain just takes over and the results are not pretty.

You are not going to like this because you too probably bought into it hook, line, and sinker, crate and barrel. But WHAT IS IT WITH THESE SHOWERS? I am not talking about rain. I have no issues with rain. Rain is fresh and life-giving and replenishing, and we get to wear our squishy rubber boots. But wedding and baby showers? Come on, what's the deal? For the sake of simplicity (though there is nothing simple about these showers), we will stick to the wedding variety for now.

I must be missing some basic genome because I really don't get it. If a women's group from Mars landed here, how would we explain this shower phenomenon? We have a colossal party with no other purpose than to gather an oversized collection of people together to collect a bunch of registry presents to prepare for a much bigger party where an even bigger shitload of presents is amassed. Intimate gatherings of a few close friends will no longer suffice. Now the guest list includes even the friend of your mother's aunt who met you when you were in Girl Scouts. Does something seem wrong with this scenario? Hello? Anyone?? Whose bright idea was this, and when did it Jump the Shark?

I poked around a little and discovered wedding showers are thought to have started in the 1890s when a hostess filled a paper parasol with small presents from the guests and turned it over the head of the bride-to-be—hence showers. We are talking trinkets here. Try doing that with the presents today, and there would be no need of a wedding since the bride would still be in intensive care with a major concussion. Can't you see that gleaming espresso machine bouncing off her beautifully coiffed noggin?

If my information is correct, showers were actually an early feminist event started as an alternative to the dowry system. They were crucial if the mother of the bride was too poor to afford a dowry or if the father was opposed to the marriage. Friends of the bride would bring her small gifts to make up for the dowry and help her walk down the aisle with the man of her choice. How romantic is that? We are not talking about silver platters from Tiffany's. This was a rejection of the patriarchal system of groom selection where Daddy had all the power. Are showers today a remnant of this transfer of power? By making sure the bride has all the goods, she controls the relationship? If the gifts are any indication, it seems she is left to control the cooking and the decorating. Is this what we women are willing to settle for?

Of course, my whining could be a case of sour grapes. I never had a shower. Not even a little one. My wedding had all of six or seven days' notice, so we were lucky to have obtained a license. Nor do I have any memory of attending any friends' showers as a young woman. Of course, in those days, we were determined to be anti-establishment. No government piece of paper or society event for us. Could this be the pendulum swinging to the opposite side? Everything is now bigger, better, and Facebook photo-ready. Now even the wedding proposal has to be a movie production.

Take this example from recent experience. About fifty people had assembled for a recent bridal shower. Soaring white spaces filled with modern sculptures set the stage in the foyer, and the living room reflected glass vistas twinkling on all sides. Sleeveless designer dresses stretched over fit, polished women—business owners, professionals, nonprofit directors, and legacy daughters. An elegantly catered buffet, mostly for display purposes, was filled with lush green salad, crab cakes, chicken salad, and, of course, dark chocolate brownies. But who is actually eating? Not these women. Yes, all appears to be perfect.

A little schmoozing, a little drinking, some food, and we were ready to get down to the important business: PRESENTS. It is time to worship at the shrine of swag, right? But one of the problems with having so many guests is so many presents. "That's a problem?" you may ask. "Isn't that the whole point?"

Each gift must be opened separately followed by the subsequent *ooos* and *ahhs* while everyone is silently judged on the "extravaganza continuum." This takes time, lots of time. Of course, knowing that there is going to be a public unveiling ups the ante. I mean, who wants to be outed as a cheapskate, having bad taste, or being simply boring?

Although we were there to watch the bride open presents that she picked out and basically ordered herself, we all just played along. Soon the balled up, silver wrapping paper climbed skyward like upscale dust bunnies, and the ribbon curled around high heels as the goods were unveiled one after the other.

148

It turns out that when asked, many women disparage the wedding shower custom until it is their turn. Suddenly they are not only believers, but they insist on even bigger production. If the attendees happen to be the lucky chosen ones—*the bridesmaids*—they also get to buy a bridesmaid's dress and matching shoes and spring for the bachelorette party. Not to mention, they must pay for a hotel room in addition to, don't forget (drum roll), the wedding present! If you are a young woman who has not or will not get married, your outlay is considerable, even enough to break your personal bank, and you never recoup the "investment." It could be pertinent to this discussion to remind you that many of these nuptial couples are already co-habituating and have their own apartments or homes complete with their own dishes and Cuisinarts. Do they really need MORE?

Who will flinch first? This whole wedding extravaganza production is like a feminine version of Ultimate Wrestling. No holds barred and go for the jugular. We have even created an entire hype about "the most important day of my life." I assure you, if you are lucky, there will be much more important days. Is there a code of silence about all this? Why isn't anyone calling for a time out, yelling STOP, SURRENDER? I can't be alone in this. Help me out here.

Maybe I should tell you about my wedding inversion theory. I am researching the thesis that the more dollars spent on the wedding, the shorter the marriage lasts. Well, okay, the formula may not work across the board, but picture Kim Kardashian and Kris Humphries (remember Kris?). They lasted 72 days and spent $16 million. Liza Minnelli and David Gest spent 4.2 million and made it to a year and a half. Or think of

Paul McCartney and Heather Mills, who spent 4.2 million and imploded before four years were up. Did anyone notice when Eddie Murphy married Tracey Edmonds? Their fourteen days of matrimony cost more than $35,000 per day.

It turns out; I am not alone in this theory. Recently, Emory University economics professors Andrew Francis and Hugo Mialon surveyed more than three thousand people, all of whom had been married just once and found that across income levels, the more you dish out on the big day, the shorter your marriage will be. Think about that for a moment. It doesn't get much clearer than that.

Let's get back to the big event. At last 4 ½ hours later, the presents were opened, the shower was over. I made my wheezing escape. My frozen smile dissolved. I survived, worn and soured, but still standing.

Now that my rant is subsiding can we move on to birthday parties?

A Rite of Passage

To inspire and guide the coming generations, we must change ourselves. Like the characters in a fairy tale; the king and queen, the princess, and the evil witch, we can find our way towards transformation and nurture this possibility in young people. Only then might we find the happily-ever-after ending.

The Challenge

Girls in the U.S. are confronted by traumatic circumstances, outrageous demands, and sensory assaults on their bodies, minds, and spirits. Coming of age in a highly sexualized, violent, media and technology-saturated, patriarchal society, they are often judged by how they look and please rather than who they are and what they achieve. They witness cynicism and hopelessness at every turn.

It no longer surprises us that the cusp of female adolescence brings a sharp rise in depression, suicide attempts, anxiety, and eating disorders. A 1996 study conducted by the American Association of University Woman shows a distinct drop in confidence for young adolescent girls.

With all the challenges of our times, it is no wonder that girls can feel disconnected from themselves and the world. Yet a sense of connection to a center of universal significance is what gives life unity and meaning. Without this connection, how can girls find answers to their crucial questions: "Who am I really?" "What is my place in the world?"

With this in mind, my friend Lin Murphy and I arranged to backpack into the woods of a nearby state park to conduct a coming-of-age ceremony for a class of 8th-grade girls. Each girl came from a unique background, but all were undergoing similar physical and emotional changes as they perched on the cusp of maturity. They knew, deep in their bones, that something important was happening to them.

Halley, one of the young participants, wrote in her journal: *"More than a mile???" I yelled, "With this thing? I can't do it. I won't do it." I had an enormous backpack already strapped on precariously, and it was threatening to tip me over. There was no response. My friends have gotten used to me shouting about things I will put up with in the end. I've always felt complaining made it better. After we had gone a while, I realized it wasn't as long as I had thought, so my mood lightened considerably. Also we had passed sheep on the way up. I love sheep. They are kind of like woolly dogs.*

The Community

Hiking into the woods, our community of cooperation is already present as the stronger girls help and wait for the slower few. After setting up camp, we began the evening of ceremony with a circle of conversation.

We asked, "What are you good at?"

They answered: Math. Being peaceful when I'm alone. Skiing. Swimming. Procrastinating. Observing. Resenting authority.

We asked, "What are you afraid of?"

They answered, Snakes. Helplessness. Confrontation. Painful death. Being lost.

We asked, "What do you wish or dream?"

They said: Being in the Olympics. Finding my way. Learning to fly through the wind. Knowing myself. Being happy.

The girls had recently begun menstruating or were soon to start. Physical and emotional changes pumped through their bodies, and their futures peeked through. We each shared a piece of our story. Lin and I talked openly about becoming women, with a determination to sweep the hidden words out of the darkness. We talked about dreams and fears. Menstruation means you have the potential to be a woman, to give birth to babies, to ideas, and to creative pursuits. You are in the process of birthing a life. As the words traveled around the circle, the meaning of menstruation changed for them from The Curse into a blessing. And womanhood took its place of power in our souls!

The Wilderness

A huge, circular meadow held us in its lush embrace. The wind breathed through the trees as the last glow of the setting sun faded quickly from the cloud-thick sky. We were alone but for the birds, the squirrels, and the voracious mosquitoes.

One by one, we blessed the girls and sent them down the meandering path. Squinting into the gathering gloom, I watched as each silent Persephone disappeared gracefully without a backward glance and the night gathered them in. Each girl hiked out to find a place of her own in the woods while I was left standing in awed silence. I felt a shiver of dread. What had we done? What if they get lost, hurt, or terror-stricken? With a deep breath and a reassuring hug, Lin and I walked back to the campfire to keep watch.

The Ceremony

Initiations can be a powerful way to assist in the transformation of a girl into a strong, inwardly-directed, courageous woman. Ceremony and ritual are the warp and woof that weave our becoming and bind us into communities. Initiations go back to the early times of all indigenous people. We find the remnants of rituals in ceremonies such as confirmation, Bar and Bat Mitzvahs, proms, and graduations. But mostly, we have abandoned initiation rituals. In their place is left an emptiness we rush to fill with work, sex, drugs, shopping, and entertainment.

Instinctually recognizing the need for modern day rites of passage, but with little to guide or inspire them, our youth go it alone. Adolescence can become a dark and lonely time of transition in which drugs and alcohol, sex, gangs, fast cars, hazing, piercing and tattoos become the tools of change. Thus teenagers often create their own rites of passage into adult life.

Joseph Campbell believed that the purpose of ritual was to carry people across difficult thresholds. These exuberant young girls were fast becoming women. By this experience of sacred celebration, perhaps we could move them towards the next doorway on their journey. I wanted to take their hands and walk part of the way beside them. I wanted them to dare greatly.

Halley wrote: *After eating dinner, we went out to the field, and our guides smudged us with sage smoke, blessed us, and sent us on our way. Some of us had no particular quest in mind. I, on the other hand, was looking for a name. Darkness fell swiftly, and I settled* *myself in. Staring up at the sky, I could see a woman in the clouds, and she was giving birth to a cloud baby!*

The Connection

Child development experts portray adolescence as a time of separation and individuation. Researchers have recently discussed another, equally important aspect: relational development or connected knowing. In relational development, women grow through connections. Often our daughters experience the hunger to connect as if they were living with a piece of themselves missing. It is a constant ache. They wonder if they truly belong to the life they are living or if they even want to. They question whether the world will be here for them as they grow up.

There is a reason that many of us are uncomfortable when we are in close proximity to adolescents. We are afraid to meet their eyes that insistently ask for answers to questions like: What are your principles? How are you living? Where do you throw your garbage? Who have you passed by on the street without seeing? Is this what you planned to become? It is difficult to be reminded of how far from grace we have fallen.

The overriding purpose of this journey into the woods is connection—connection to each other, to the community, to the earth, to the Great Mystery, and ultimately to one's deepest self.

The Elders

That night in the woods was also an initiation for me. Guiding young girls brings me into eldering. Me, an elder! Somehow this ageing snuck up on me when I wasn't looking and bit me on the stretch-marked rear-

155

end. As these beautiful, young girls begin their menstrual cycles, I am looking toward menopause. That night the prospect of growing older and perhaps wiser appeared to be a blessing and a sacred responsibility.

Shaila: *I pray for guidance, I hope for guidance, I wish for guidance, and yet at the time I had no idea why I would need the guidance. Later that night, I realized why. I danced in my circle of protection in the woods. My head started to sink into the ground, then my upper torso, followed by my legs, then my feet, all departing the earth, underground. I sank deeper, and deeper. I began to take root; roots came forth from my fingers, my toes, my hair almost into a tree growing horizontally. My circle protected me. I trusted it with my faith in life, in the spirit. I cried afraid and alone. Then I heard it --- the far distant beating of the drum calling me back.*

A Bushmen elder said, "There are three signs of a culture without rites of passage: 1) There are no elders. 2) The adults are confused. 3) The youth are violent." We need leaders who can point the way. And some of us can now strive to take our place as the elders. We can be there to beckon and welcome the coming generations preparing to become adults.

The Return

After the night slowly eased into a new dawn, it was time to rejoin civilization. We were greeted by a beautiful luncheon prepared by the mothers to welcome their girls, tired and dusty, back home. There were hugs, hurried stories, and a lingering feeling that maybe, just maybe, something had changed.

Sabbath Nights

Sometime in our early 30's, Lee and I decided something was missing. Please don't misunderstand; it was a good life. Lee had a job he found both challenging and satisfying. I was part of a supportive playgroup that was soon to grow into my starting a Waldorf School. We had a son, a daughter, and a new one on the way. Our pre-revolutionary house was slowly transforming into a real home. We gardened, walked, and meditated.

We had already settled on the major holiday celebrations: the Jewish New Year in September, then Thanksgiving, followed by a Christmas-Chanukah mash-up, then Passover, and a big Summer Solstice happening and, of course, birthdays along the way. Yet there remained a gap. With various commitments, schedules, and lessons to coordinate, our days were hectic, and the weeks rolled on. By the time Friday evening came around, we were ready to collapse, switch gears, and touch base again.

Magically, the light dawned, or rather the flame flickered. What about the Sabbath? Lee and I are both Jewish, but our religious educations were minimal at best. The only idea I had about Friday night Sabbath celebration came from a scene in *Fiddler on the Roof*. So I called up an old friend of the family, and with pencil poised, I asked, "How do you do the Sabbath?"

With the *Fiddler on the Roof* soundtrack playing and plenty of enthusiasm, we began. Ideally, the house is cleaned, challah is baked, and a tablecloth and candlesticks grace the table. We prepare a good meal, though it can be simple, with, perhaps, a special desert. We often stayed home on Friday night, so we could transform it into family time, a chance to unwind from the week and give thanks for our blessings. Of course, we should attempt to do this all week long—when should we not sing God's praises? But the truth is, we forget. So on this one night each week, we create a tiny, sacred space for our family in order to invite in the sacred.

We begin by kindling the Sabbath lights. These are the beeswax candles that Lee makes every winter. Somehow the eyes of our ancestors, of Abraham, Leah, and Moses seem to be winking at us from those flames. And then we sing:

> *May the Lord protect and defend you*
> *May He always shield you from shame*
> *May you come to be*
> *In Israel a shining name*
> *May God bless you and grant you long lives*
> *May the Lord fulfill our Sabbath prayer for you*

After the blessing over the wine (or apple cider) and bread, we go around the table and each gives thanks for one thing from the week. It can be our visiting guest, something that happened, the people here, or the ones who are missed. But on particularly hungry days, it is for the food itself. There are often too many jokes and lots of commentary until we make it all around the table. One night, our young daughter was searching desperately for something to say. Her eyes scanned the table, and she triumphantly proclaimed, "I am grateful for silverware!" At last, we joined hands around the table. "Blessings on the meal!"

Many friends and guests have shared in our Sabbath as the years have gone by. Our children's friends all grew to expect it and looked forward to it. It seems to act as an anchor and a comfort. Not bad for a little tradition. I guess we benefit from the 6,000 years of history that guides our little Sabbath. Perhaps our ancestors are even now sharing in the blessings.

Okonomiyaki Recipe

This is a meal that sometimes ends up on our Sabbath table. We found this recipe in the first *Moosewood Cookbook,* by Molly Katzen. Its roots are in the wonderful Moosewood Restaurant in Ithaca, New York, where my sister-in-law Elyn used to work. Her stories about those early days are epic! The place was, in 1977, the forerunner of a new way of cooking that arose out of all of us hippies and newly converted vegetarians. It was run as a collective, and all these years later, it still is! In those days, people began to realize that there were other things to eat besides meat and potatoes and one overcooked vegetable. There was delectable cuisine from every country throughout the world. Amazing!

Early on, we were inspired by Adelle Davis, who wrote many books about the detriments of food processing and food additives. Francis Moore Lappe came along not long after with *Diet for a Small Planet.* We thought this book would change the world, and, perhaps, in some ways, it did.

After making this dish once when our children were small, it became a welcome tradition in our family. It is another one of those what's-left-in-the-refrigerator meals. Later I did some research in Japan, and discovered that there really is an art to traditional Okonomiyaki, but this recipe is not it. If you want authenticity, find some real Japanese instructions, but if you want an easy, quick vegetarian meal, here it is.

Ingredients

- 1 cup flour (you can mix in a little chickpea or almond flour)
- 2/3 cup water
- 1 teaspoon of salt

161

- 1 teaspoon baking powder
- 3 eggs
- 1 and 1/2 cups shredded cabbage
- 3 carrots, grated
- 1 zucchini, grated
- 4 kale leaves, remove ribs and cut in small ribbons
- Green onions, chopped
- Any other veggies (corn, red peppers, spinach) shredded or chopped

Preparation

In a large bowl, whisk together the flour and water until smooth. Beat in the eggs. Add the cabbage and the other vegetables. Mix the batter but not too much. Drop the batter by the spoonful into the hot oil on a skillet or griddle. Make sure they are browned and cooked through, the way you would cook pancakes.

Sauce: We dip these into tamari with ginger root grated into it. But you can also use mayonnaise or BBQ sauce or the Japanese style dipping sauce below:

Mix together:

- ¼ cup Ketchup
- ¼ cup mustard
- 1 tablespoon Worchester sauce
- 1 tablespoon rice wine
- 1 tablespoon tamari
- 1 tablespoon honey mixed with grated ginger

Growing Side By Side

I just opened my heart and I fell in love with everyone here. I am leaving a place where you could be whoever you want to be. This is my family.

Jerome, journal entry

Imagine a gathering place where young adults from different backgrounds and beliefs come together to create a working community. There they are encouraged to develop their own unique talents, and become, in Cornell West's words, "prisoners of hope." Surrounded by organic gardens and rolling green lawns, they pick fresh vegetables for their meals, discuss issues of race and privilege, and develop ways to guide the young children who will arrive for a summer camp program.

Side By Side is a leadership program that uses the arts and community service to create change. Located on a small college campus in upstate New York, its mission is to cultivate leadership skills, foster social awareness, and inspire hope in young people between the ages of 17 and 22. These Youth Leaders participate in an intensive training week followed by two weeks of running an overnight camp for underserved city children. Allow me to introduce you to two of its past participants.

Jerome is a young Latino man of 20 from the South Bronx. He dresses in baggy jeans and a football jersey and is strong but reserved, maybe even skeptical. He has spent his life in and out of foster care. After belonging to a gang for many years, he recently found his way to a community organization in Harlem where he works with the younger boys. That program sent him to Side By Side; he assumed it would be an easy summer job.

Robin is a tough-looking white girl from LA who is here because her mother sent her. Robin hopes it might not be totally boring. Dressed in tight black clothes with lots of chain jewelry, she will be a senior at her all-white, private school in the fall. Robin takes music and dance lessons and enjoys many other privileges of education and wealth. She is also used to the spotlight and watches the activities with cool skepticism.

My Story. Your Story. Our Story.

Each youth leader shares their life story in the ceremonial circle. Jerome tells his story with brisk honesty, revealing to the group that his mother is an addict and he never knew his father. He tells the group he had no one who truly cared about him except his grandmother. She died last year of diabetes. Jerome describes joining the gang and feeling that it was finally a place where he belonged. The group listens closely and thoughtfully to Jerome's story.

The following morning, he asks to speak again: *Every day since my grandma died I woke up with a weight in my chest. I didn't want to get out of bed. This morning, after telling all of you my story, I woke up and felt so happy, I jumped out of bed! The weight was gone.*

Robin wrote in her journal:

Listening to Jerome's biography was quite an experience for me. I have never had, and can't imagine ever having, the strength to look at myself that deeply. The way he actually showed himself and made it clear what he thought of himself was impressive. Our society has me so deeply trained to show only certain sides of myself that I sometimes doubt the existence of any other side.

What is going on here? On a 95-degree summer day when smart people are in air- conditioned rooms sipping iced tea, young people at Side By Side are working 14-hour days for no pay. These are not your typical teenagers. Instead of hanging out, they are telling their life stories, discussing race and privilege, writing in journals. They have various goals, face widely different challenges, and enjoy a variety of tastes in food and music, but they all want to make a difference in the world.

Growing Community

Robin writes: *The group of youth leaders became a very powerful community. Having the kids there was important because we all had to get along just to be able to work with the kids and make a camp happen. And we did it!*

165

Journal exercise: Conversation in color

There is a need, an actual longing, in our world for community. We see this longing go awry in gangs, raves, hazing, and in the high rates of teen depression. Forming community involves a process of coming together to create a sense of belonging, of being connected to others and to ideas and values that make our lives meaningful. Strong community can remedy the isolation and helplessness of modern life. Author and educator Parker Palmer explains, "The truth we are seeking is the truth that lies ultimately in the community of being where we not only know, but are known." As the Side By Side staff and youth leaders work and play together, listen to each other, and share their art and writing, a caring community blossoms.

Robin: *We were all from drastically different backgrounds but able to offer and receive different things. It was this cultural exchange that made us a group.*

Diversity: Shades of Difference

Struggling with issues of racism and how to understand differences is always a challenge, but it was made easier by the growing trust of a caring community. The activities, the meals, the free time, and the shared tasks all became a place to explore differences and similarities. After an evening watching a powerful film about racism, we discovered that we do not have to agree, but can try to listen with kindness and respect.

Jerome: *I realized that there are a lot of people who have no idea about racism. Robin, for instance, really tested me. She wasn't educated about black people. She never really knew any. But I appreciated that she was trying to learn. She wanted to step in and take some kind of action. That really touched me.*

The young men and women of color share their many confrontations with racial profiling. Questions are asked, and at the end of that long night, there is an openness that wasn't there previously.

Robin: *No one actually talks about racism the way we talked about it. To have someone who had become my friend tell of his actual experiences with prejudice made it real. Then you know that we must do something to change things.*

Jerome: *I don't think I ever had white people listen to me before.*

Service: The Campers Arrive

Marian Wright Edelman, founder and director of the Children's Defense Fund, says that "service is the rent we pay for living." Community service is living proof that we can make a difference in the world. Becoming involved in community service is not the only way to make this happen, but it may be the best option available to young people. In the words of Julia Butterfly Hill after she climbed a redwood tree as a teenager and did not climb back down to earth until she was an adult three years later, "We will win some and we will lose some, but what else would we want to do with our lives but offer them in service to the world."

Once the campers arrive, Robin and Jerome are busy every waking moment. Opportunities for service are endless at Side by Side's summer camp. There are activities to arrange, safety to maintain, mouths to feed, games to play, fights to referee, and homesickness to ease. Everyone is exhausted but exhilarated by week's end.

Closing the Circle
We ended the three weeks with a closing circle.

Robin: *I feel as if I've been awakened. I am inspired to work with children. I have more confidence. Just the fact that I could go through that is huge. I look back and think—that was my best.*

Jerome: *I didn't expect much, but I just started opening my heart to everybody, and I fell in love with everyone*

168

here. I am leaving a place where you could be whoever you wanted to be. This is my family!

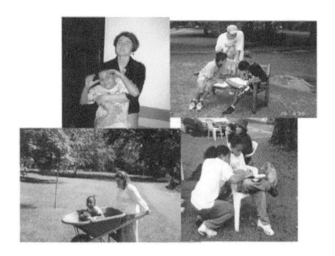

Jerome, who became a leader in the group, and Robin give us a glimpse of the hope and excitement that thrives in a community where personal transformation and social change occur. It is not about knowing all the wrongs in the world; it is about knowing what we can make right. It is growing side by side.

Family in the '80s

Top: Robert and Samantha Nagel.
Bottom: Kilimanjaro January 1ˢᵗ 1996

Top: Side by Side Program
Bottom: Girl's Rite of Passage

BLOSSOMS

Phoenix Rising

Changes come in many forms. Some sneak up on you from behind when you are distracted by an untied shoelace or a pile of dirty dishes. Others come like a sprite in the night urging you to pack your bags and move to Sedona. Sometimes change saunters in like an unemployed hustler in cowboy boots and has his way with you. Not being a particularly subtle woman, I seem to get the version of change that hits you over the head with a frying pan and squawks, "Yoo- hoo, move your butt over here."

I have heard it said that the world will end in fire, and one night in the middle of autumn in my 50th year, I got a first-hand look at that scorching form of change. My house burned down. Well, not *down* exactly, more like up.

One quiet Sunday evening, I went to bed completely engrossed in my ordinary, albeit frenzied, life replete with shoulds, musts, and highly significant ought-tos. My appointment book eagerly rested on the table brimming with expectations. Yet, only a few hours later, I was bedless, clothesless, homeless, and appointment-free.

Here's what I had previously thought: If I ever was involved in a fire, first I'd get the kids out of the house, then the animals. If there was any time left, I'd go for the photo albums. The people and the animals is a no-brainer. And the "save the photo albums" plan sounds simple, right? Well, think again. After raising four kids and various additions for twenty-seven years, it is not as easy as simply tucking them under your arms and running out of the house. Even for this sporadic chronicler, I had a lot of pictures. Sixteen photo albums do not easily fit under two arms. There I was—my house burning down—and I stood in the hall with one album tucked under each arm and fourteen to go. What should I have done? I moved towards the guestroom away from the fire and tried to think. What if the whole house burned down? Better not keep them in the house. I figured I would dump them out the back door. Uh-oh. The fire hoses might soak them. I stood there swaying with indecision. Finally I raced to the back door, dumped out the recyclables, loaded in the photo albums and dragged the bin out into the yard.

I was doing great, but that was as far as I got. The children, the pets, and the photo albums were safe, but what next? I turned towards the shelves of books, and it hit me; I was going to lose all of them. My life was in those shelves. All the books on childbirth, gardening, and environmental issues, an entire shelf on Waldorf education, and the books on women's issues and healing guides stared back at me helplessly. The accounts of Native Americans, religion, a huge collection of fairy and folk tales, another of poetry waited for their demise. I couldn't forget the biographies and the novels! The ones I loved and passed on to my sons and daughters: *The Lion the Witch and the Wardrobe, Siddhartha, Grapes of Wrath, The Bean Trees, A Story Like the Wind, House of Spirits*. I took a deep breath and whispered, "You were terrific. I have loved you, but now I bid you goodbye."

Suddenly I felt like I was floating. I had so many clothes, I couldn't decide what to wear in the morning. I had too many electrical gadgets—toasters, juicers, waffle irons, boomboxes, and answering machines. Those things were not me, and I realized I could do

175

without them. In that moment, I pictured myself setting forth into the rest of my life free and unfettered with nothing to tie me down or fray my soul.

If I were a bona fide flower child, my story would end here, and I would be living in a yurt on the ashes of my old house with a few charred pots and a warm sleeping bag dispensing wisdom in short, easily digestible segments. The truth is a lot messier and much less picturesque. My books survived, though they were a bit wet and smelly. The house did not burn down; it merely burned. It did not turn into purified dry ash to blow away in the wind, but to a sodden, reeking mess. The alchemy failed; my lead did not turn into gold, it merely melted. My life was not liberated and simplified but complicated and inconvenienced.

"We will live simply," my sometimes simple-minded husband said, "we don't need much." I wanted him to explain to me how to live simply with three jobs, two offices, doctoral thesis deadlines, volunteer responsibilities, three rental units, a hungry teenager, two cats, a dog, and a turtle? Someone better break it to him gently; those carefree Woodstock days were long gone.

Did I mention my research papers? I was close to the final approach on my doctoral thesis. To this glorious end, I had amassed a box of floppy discs and a three-foot stack of photocopied research articles sorted by categories. Most of these survived the fire (yay!) but not the fire hoses (boo!). I despaired at the damp, smelly, mess. The following night over sushi, the man in the next booth told me to put them in the freezer; it would stop the rotting process and buy me some time.

Thank goodness for good friends. I arrived at Jane's house dragging two garbage bags filled with sticky, crumbling papers. They fit perfectly between the pop tarts and the turkey where they waited until I was settled in a rental house with an oven. I then began to peel and bake my papers in small stacks. Just as with pancakes, the skill is in the flipping. Flip too soon, and the dampness will cause mildew. Flip too late, and the smell of charred paper fills the house and destroys the appetite. If you opened the office closet and inhaled, you would find my resurrected research.

Friends asked how our 14-year-old son was doing. I didn't know. After the first confused weeks sleeping in various places, he seemed completely unaffected. He was involved in his own life, and this did not seem to place that high on his personal Richter scale. That is, until one day almost two months after the fire, when he said, "You know what I really miss?" I thought, *Oh boy, here it comes at last. He has buried this for so long.*

"No, what is it honey?" I asked with tender parental concern.

"Tall glasses," he answered from the depths of his soul.

"Tall glasses?" I gulped in confusion.

"Yup. The glasses we have here are too small for a good drink."

Okay, so much for deep inner healing. Maybe he really was okay. I soon located a couple of tall glasses for his liquid pleasure.

Annie Lamont says that courage is fear that has said its prayers. Maybe twenty-four years of family songs and prayers, tears and laughter, joys and sorrows under those 250-year-old living room beams counted for something because we never felt afraid. This is not a story of tragedy. Tragedy is babies suffering. Tragedy is mothers dying young. Tragedy is planes crashing and buildings crumbling. This fire was not a tragedy. I keep searching for a word that is stronger than inconvenience, but less than disaster. Instead I am left with the words of a well-fed bear—"Oh bother."

Maybe this will become the story of the phoenix, the one that rises from the ashes, dusts herself off, spreads her wings, and flies off into the sunset. There I was in the second half of my life, my children mostly grown, expectations becoming clearer, life settling into comfortable routines, and I got this wake-up call in the middle of the night. Okay. I was wide awake. I was paying attention. I saw friends who rallied support with food, blankets, and all their extra attic furniture. I saw a family unified and ready to celebrate. I saw a husband who made each drama into the latest new adventure. I saw blessings everywhere I turned. I saw how transformation crept into the roofless house of my being and pushed me out to greet it.

So watch out for me. I rose from the ashes — dusty and a wee bit discombobulated — but ready to fly. Next time, I will ask for ice instead of fire, or at least a brick house. But until then, this fire will definitely suffice.

Roses are Red

Roses are red
Violets are blue
I'm looking for romance
Where are you?

I've located the slinky lingerie and the long-stemmed red roses. Now all I need is a little more imagination. This holiday does not always come easy. For those of you who have no special honeybun or who, like me, have a well-used one, it can be a challenge to get in the Valentine's Day spirit.

How are you facing Valentine's Day this year—with breathless anticipation or with shudders of dread? Last year, 192 million cards and more than 2.5 million roses were exchanged on this one holiday alone. That's a lot of sincere gestures. I wonder if we are using them to say what really matters. Perhaps if we defined love more expansively by taking it out of the exclusive realm of romantic, usually sexual, love, we could honor the people who touch our lives with caring and kindness. Then we might create a different kind of Valentine's Day.

I remember when I was pregnant with my second child. My husband, son, and I were a perfect three some, and I wondered how I could add another to our world. But then my daughter burst onto our scene, and I began to grasp something: unlike French fries or dollars in my wallet, love is infinite. The more you love, the more you create a fertile ground for good loving. It's like the magic porridge pot, always remaining full no matter how many times you dip in.

Anthropologist, Helen Fischer, found that people "madly in love" had loads of dopamine in their brain. I

179

remember that rush. It is why couples on the roller coaster of new love can stay up all night and still have the energy to dip strawberries in chocolate the next morning. But this level of love cannot last, and it's probably just as well because the dishes would never get done or the taxes get paid. If we're lucky, the passion moves on to become connection, which releases oxytocin and gives us a wonderful feeling of well-being. That's why people with partners and friends live longer, healthier lives. Okay so forget about the satin boxers and the edible body oil, my husband may have to settle for snuggles on the couch. After all, it's really gratitude not bling that delivers happiness. Grateful people report higher levels of life satisfaction; they exercise more and are healthier. And experiences make people much happier than accumulating stuff does.

Regardless, this year I am making a list of all my true loves. On the list are my nieces, my sister-in law, and the neighbors who bring me a bag of apples or a new plant for the garden. There is even a sweet mechanic who keeps my ancient Subaru on the road. They have all earned their place. My dear friend Lin who boosts my spirits and, of course, Kuma, my excessively loyal dog, are both there. The list keeps expanding. I add my mostly-grown kids who share their fascinating lives with me—some of the time. And, oh yes, my hottie husband is on there too. Hmmm, I can already feel the glow of wellbeing spreading as the calories melt away.

It's time for the new Valentine's Day audit—six degrees of connection. It can improve your life and make the world a better place. In 1987, Martin Luther King, Jr. reminded us that "We are caught in an inescapable network of mutuality, tied in a single garment of destiny. Whatever affects one directly, affects all indirectly." Let's strengthen that web. Go find someone who has touched you this year and wish them a Happy Valentine's Day.

Hummus With Love Recipe

Instead of chocolate or ecologically toxic flowers that poison many young women farm workers in Central America, you might want to share a little hummus with the people you love. It is, after all, a very sexy food.

Historians say that hummus, from the Arabic word for chickpeas, predates writing. People have been making and eating it for more than 10,000 years. In the Middle East, it is as common and as necessary as ketchup is here. It could even be a tool for diplomacy. Make hummus, not war! In fact, some people swear that it is an aphrodisiac! *Make love, not war. And eat hummus!*

You can't go wrong with hummus. As an appetizer, a sandwich spread, or an ingredient for a great mid-eastern dinner, make sure a bowl of hummus is on hand. And if people drop in unexpectedly and they have that famished look, excuse yourself for all of six minutes and come back with a few carrots and a bowl of hummus. You'll be able to bask in the general satisfaction of the room. Once again for the following recipe, I never actually measure anything, but it always seems to work.

Ingredients

- 2 cups drained well-cooked or canned chickpeas, liquid reserved
- 1/2 cup tahini (sesame paste)
- 1/4 cup extra-virgin olive oil, plus oil for drizzling
- 2 cloves garlic, peeled
- Salt and freshly ground black pepper to taste and a splash of tamari
- 1 teaspoon ground cumin
- 1 tablespoon paprika, plus a sprinkling for garnish
- Juice of 1 or 2 lemons
- Fresh parsley or cilantro leaves
- Optional: Celery leaves, red pepper slices, chives or green onions or some grated beets (for a lovely pink shade!)

Preparation

1. Put everything in a food processor and begin to process
2. Taste and adjust. Serve, drizzled with the olive oil and sprinkled with a bit more paprika and some parsley.

Let Them Eat Meat

The story begins with a call from the storyteller: *Crik*—and then the resounding *Crak* from the audience. It is a old-style call and response, a tradition dating back thousands of years. *Crik* offers a story; *Crak* announces a readiness to listen.

Once upon a time many years ago, Anansi, the trickster—part spider, part man— had all the wisdom of the world stored in one pot. All of it. You see, Nyami, the sky God, had given the pot of wisdom to Anansi and instructed him to share it with all the peoples of the world. Anansi carried that pot with him and looked in it every day. It was chockful of wonderful ideas like how to grow food, build houses, and stay warm. But wouldn't you know it, the more Anansi gazed at that wisdom, the more he wanted to keep it for himself. Anansi was greedy, and so he decided to hide the wisdom away from the world.

Picture, if you can, a land that time forgot; where people are generous and gentle and strive for justice, where they have little but share much. Once upon a time, I arrived in Kafunda, a learning village just outside of Harare, the capital of Zimbabwe. This is an intentional community where sustainable rural life practices and collaborative change form the foundation for the future.

We stepped down from the van into a starry night populated with brightly wrapped women bursting into song, their swaying hips and throaty voices enfolding us. What a welcome! After a quick tour of red

185

adobe thatched roof buildings that were the dining hall, dorms, meeting rooms, and library, we turned to examine the mini tikki lodges, or composting toilets, gracefully swathed in bamboo. We would soon get to know them rather intimately as they were the cornerstone of Kafunda's teaching. Villagers came here to learn how to build a composting toilet, thus shifting the conversation from one of poverty to one of capacity and possibility. This is a learning village where people strive to imagine and develop vibrant communities of the future. Like an overflowing pot of wisdom, Kafunda seeps into the far corners of Zimbabwe and keeps on spreading. Anansi, the spider, must be nearby.

After a few days of the daily routine, I was falling in love. It felt like a fairytale. We'd meet each day in the thatch-covered, open-air hall where everyone practiced the art of conversation and where group discussions were conducted with participation and civility to maximize the collective intelligence. In these conversations, diverse viewpoints were welcomed. The goal was to transform conflict into creative cooperation. Kafunda believed that transformative change for the common good called for personal involvement, collective wisdom, and co-creation in order to discover new solutions. People who were involved would then take ownership and responsibility for action.

This sounds like Utopia. Sigh. But remember, in any good story, the wicked stepmother or evil wizard must appear. Even in Kafunda, all was not perfect. With a *Crik* the stories were gathered in, with a *Crak* we began to see the challenges and imperfections.

Crik: Once upon a time, there was a beautiful country of elephants and maize fields, of awe-inspiring

Victoria Falls south of where Stanley found Livingston, I presume. The people played soccer, and hospitality was as natural as a deep breath. They asked, "Wakadii?" How are you? And responded, "Ndiripo kana wakadiiwo." I am fine if you are fine. With each greeting, the people reminded us that we are all interconnected. "How did you sleep?" they asked. "If you did not sleep well, how could I sleep well?" This was "it takes a village" in action.

Crak: In 1980, after years of civil war with Great Britain, Robert Mugabe, Zimbabwe's heroic freedom fighter, was elected prime minister amid great hope for the newly independent nation. He would lead Rhodesia, a brutally colonized nation to its new start as Zimbabwe. Just imagine, if you can, Bob Marley singing "Zimbabwe," a song he wrote at the government's invitation for the country's independence. Hope was a shining commodity. But over the past thirty years, those hopes have been dashed. Mugabe, charged with numerous human rights abuses, has run the economy of his own nation into the ground. Though Mugabe has grown old and rich, Zimbabwe's 11 million people have faced rampant inflation, 70% unemployment, starvation, malnutrition, and desperate poverty. The inflation rate rose to almost 8,000%, the world's highest. It is said that it requires a wheelbarrow of paper dollars to buy a loaf of bread.

With frequent power and water outages, drinking water became unreliable, and dysentery and cholera swept through as the health of the civilian population floundered. By 1997 25% of the population of Zimbabwe had been infected by HIV AIDS. And Mugabe refused to even acknowledge this, let alone take preventative action.

After Mugabe ordered forcible land redistribution, there was a mass migration of white Zimbabweans out of Zimbabwe; many were professionals and experienced farmers. Since then, the country has experienced a severe shortage of doctors, nurses, and teachers and debilitating food shortages, turning the "breadbasket of Africa" into one of Africa's most food-insecure states. Amnesty International says there are "massive human rights problems that have been going on for years."

Crik: Rocks reared up along our path like giant sleeping elephants under a magic spell. Long green grass and massive boulders surrounding thatched roof, open-aired buildings produced a movie-like setting. We formed a circle where each speaker told their story. Kafunda call this "harvesting conversations that matter."

Anna, a tiny hummingbird of a woman, dressed in traditional African dress and headscarf, was a widow. She spoke softly with a downturned gaze. "I could not provide for my children, and I thought I had nothing to offer—no talents, no skills, and no intelligence. I was so sad."

After training at Kafunda, she became a village leader and founded God's Power, a knitting cooperative. She was a dynamic, motivational speaker. She looked up, her voice gaining strength as she proudly displayed sweaters for sale.

At 19, Ronald was tall, thin, and self-contained. He watched quietly until he was asked about trees.

Then he became animated as he told how he learned about tree planting, which is crucial to the prevention of erosion and drought. He directed a tree-planting project and traveled throughout the area. He dreamed of going to university.

Phillip was dressed impeccably in a threadbare suit. He was a dignified, older man new to the area. Recently, he had become a small landowner as part of Mugabe's redistribution and farmed a small parcel of land with his son. With bursting pride, he described the organic methods and composting techniques he learned at Kafunda. Then he quietly asked, "What can organic methods do against a continent-wide drought?" What could we answer? Severe drought has been spreading each year in Africa caused mainly by global climate change and deforestation.

Crak: I sat at a table in the dining room with Brigitta, a bright-eyed 20-year old. She quietly wept as she described her sister's recent suicide. Brigitta's sister was very ill, having been infected with HIV by her husband. Their two children were HIV positive, and her husband had already remarried and infected another wife. Although Sub-Saharan Africa is only 10% of the world's population, it contains 60% of all the people living with AIDS. Every day, the equivalent of three 9/11's-worth of people die from this epidemic. *Every day!* Zimbabwe has one of the highest rates of HIV and AIDS in the world. One in every three people is infected, dropping the average lifespan down to 31 years. AIDS is orphaning an entire generation of children. Young people between the ages of 15 and 24 make up approximately half of all new infections, with girls and young women being particularly vulnerable.

A brightly dressed woman told how her husband infected her with the virus. She waits to hear if her newborn, curled contentedly in my arms, is also HIV positive. She told me his name is Rufasha, which means "it is enough" since she wants no more children. She needed to feed him formula so that her breast milk would not infect him, but there was none to be found. There is very little AID's prevention or treatment but plenty of shame and pretending. Brigitta, her beautiful young face shining with tears, turned to me, the American, for answers. But I had only questions.

Crik: There are also many wonders in this tale. I was invited to Rusape, a small city eighty miles south of the capital, for a home stay. Hilda was my host. She gave me her bed while she slept on the stone kitchen floor. In a spotless white blouse and cheerful head scarf, she proudly directed me to the composting toilet in her yard.

Hilda founded the widow's group. When the men of the village forbade their wives to go study in Kafunda, the widows stepped boldly forward. "We had no men to tell us no," she told me. And thus, Hilda and some others set out on the two-day walk to Kafunda. They returned with the knowledge and supplies to each build a composting toilet. Now the headman sits in on Kafunda celebrations and takes credit for the composting toilets in his village.

You might wonder what is so important about a basic cement and thatch composting toilet, but it is actually crucial. In some places, there is only one poorly maintained, communal toilet. It only takes being without an available or functioning toilet for a few hours to see that it might be more important than

190

money. Without them, people are forced to relieve themselves off every path, which soon leads to people stepping in it, tracking it home, and getting sick from it. Dysentery exists in epic proportions and diarrhea is a leading killer of children, under age 5 in Africa.

The moment Anansi decided to keep the pot of wisdom, his worries began. "What if someone tries to steal it?" he fretted. "I need to find somewhere to hide it." He decided to stash it at the top of a tree. Holding the pot full of knowledge, he started to climb the towering Baobab tree. Struggling to balance the pot with one hand, he climbed with the other. His progress was painstakingly slow.

Nelson Mandela said, "Millions of people in the world's poorest countries remain trapped in the prison of poverty. It is time to set them free." We cannot solve poverty, starvation, and illness, let alone AIDS, without creating healthy economies. Here in the United States, we are used to supersized meals, endless new clothes, and mounds of garbage tossed out weekly. We have McMansions popping up like spring dandelions as our dumps expand and our carbon dioxide output destroys the world. Which country needs fixing?

The emergency aid industry spends $70 billion per year on aid with little lasting impact on Africa. Some believe that it is not aid but rather trade that is needed. USA and Europe deny Africa access to their markets. If Africa gained a mere 1% of the world's share of exports, it would be worth five times the total amount of foreign aid it receives. Let's be honest here. We, the Western world, decimated Africa—first with the slave trade, followed by Colonialism where we mined every resource in sight. Then we marched in WHO and WTO, and now they struggle against AIDs and global climate change. While African countries continue to finance the western world through fifteen billion dollar annual debt service, thousands of African children die each day from easily preventable malnutrition and disease. So whose policies need to be improved?

Anansi's son watched as his father slowly climbed. Finally, the youngster said, "You know, if you tie the pot to your back, it will be easier to climb the tree." Anansi, hearing this advice, flew into a rage.

"What nerve! A youngster with a bit of common sense thinks he knows more than I who has the whole pot of wisdom." In his fury, the pot slipped and fell, shattering on the ground. Anansi watched as the pieces of wisdom flew in every direction.

"Such a mess," he declared as he threw his now empty hands up in the air and swung away into the forest.

Soon, villagers found bits of wisdom scattered about. Some placed a shard in their pocket; others took a little piece home. And that is how it is to this day. No one person, not even Anansi, has all the wisdom. But whenever people gather together to share and exchange ideas, there wisdom exists and expands!

What will I do with this African experience? Will I go home, back to porcelain flushing toilets and organic salads, and like the rest of the world, slowly forget about Zimbabwe? Or am I ready to relinquish some luxuries so that the *third* world can become part of the *real* world? Perhaps like Anansi, I am complicit in hoarding knowledge (and resources and opportunity).

I baked a cake for our last days' celebration. We walked a mile to procure three eggs, and found some flour in the back of an empty cupboard. One of the women brought a little butter. I had a bar of chocolate and some nuts in my bags. Then I discovered two tiny zucchinis in the otherwise empty larder. Everything went in, and it somehow miraculously became a cake. That seems to be the way of life here, making due amid huge challenges and tiny miracles.

Before departing for home, we formed a community circle. As I said goodbye, words came out slowly, and joys and tears intermingle like sadza, the traditional porridge of cornmeal and water.

Crik Crak

In Zimbabwe, there is a saying about an unusual white beetle. Upon finding such a beetle, a person will exclaim, "I shall eat meat today!" It is good luck, like a four-leaf clover. Many here no longer dare to hope. They have seen too much loss and sorrow in the past and too few opportunities in their future. People in the United States dream of winning the million-dollar lottery, but in Zimbabwe, they dream simply of eating meat for a day.

When I returned home, Brigitta continued to communicate with me. Despite her knowledge of the disease, she became pregnant by a boyfriend who infected her with HIV. She delivered a baby, all alone, with no money for hospital bills or HIV treatment, and, of course, no money for that education she had once imagined for herself. The baby is now a toddler.

Here are some excerpts from her letters and emails to me:

How are you my dearest? We all fine. Baby is recovering well after she almost drowned in sewer tank. Now underweight have got worms because of dirty water. Bye and miss you.

How did it happen? I ask.

My dearest, she fell into it. The original lids were stolen for the whole street, so we put temporary lids and put stones on top. I don't know who removed the stones— whether it was the other older kids or what. She was saved by a three-year-old kid who came telling me she had entered into the drainage. Had it been two minutes, she could have died. When I first saw her, thought she was dead, there floating on top. How? I don't know. The vision and memory still fresh. It was terrible. Anyway good news is that she has recovered. Yeah elections over, things not yet normalized, no money on the market yet. I cannot explain really what I am doing but we are surviving. Well got to go, I love you.

We are doing just fine my dearest. We at home. Electricity just gone. Sitting in the dark.

My dearest, had been at my deceased sister's father in-law. People are sick. All of the family members are positive, the brothers, sisters, and their wives. The other brother and wife had stroke and is in wheelchair and cannot talk. My sister's kid has been in and out of the hospital but has survived ten years positive since mother died. They don't know my situation and asked me to take care of her since they are all are sick. Two of my only brothers are also infected. The elder one is now sick. Eva do you have anything about curses and how to break them? I feel this is not what I made my life to be. Something is very wrong with the situation that is not what I planned! How are you?

I think Martin Luther King, Jr. knew about sharing the pot of wisdom when he accepted the Nobel Peace prize in 1964 and said, "I have the audacity to believe that peoples everywhere can have three meals a day for their bodies, education and culture for their minds, and dignity, equality, and freedom for their spirits. I still believe that we shall overcome."

Anansi's shards of wisdom are still waiting to be found by all of us. Together, we can share them with all the peoples of the world, and we shall, indeed we must, overcome.

To Every Season, Turn, Turn, Turn

To My Grandson upon his arrival on earth

August 20, 1998

Dear Jyasi Aaron,

At last, this is it! Today is the day you begin your journey to earth. What a day you have chosen—a summer day in August. The smell of sun-kissed fruit fills the sultry air. The birds are singing. I woke at 6 AM wondering about you. We have been waiting all of August, each day making our plans around the possibility of your arrival. Your Aunt Shanti came all the way from Kentucky to take care of you. She waited patiently for two weeks, but you were shy. Yesterday she had to fly back. Today you will begin the journey.

To everything there is a season,
turn, turn, turn

You speak to us of patience. "What's the rush? Why is everyone so uptight and anxious?" You said, "Chill. There is a time, to every purpose under heaven." Each day throughout this month, I found myself wondering who you might be? Already you have changed many lives. Why were you called down to earth? I may not be wise or psychic enough to answer those questions, but I know one thing for sure: you are coming with a priceless gift for me—my new title of GRANDMOTHER. I have been secretly trying it on to see if it fits.

On this bright morning, I feel energized, as if I could do everything! I clean the house so you will feel welcome. I email the extended family that we are still waiting. I step into the garden and imagine you squatting next to me digging in the warm earth asking me questions about worms. "How do they breathe under all that dirt? Is it true that both halves will become a whole worm if I cut this one with the shovel?" In yoga class, I picture how I will hold you in my arms and gaze into your curious, probing eyes. I prepare a big pot of corn chowder to feed all the people who will gather for your birth and imagine us making cookies together. Do you prefer chocolate chip cookies or peanut butter? Finally, before the sun sets, I take dogs, yours and mine, for a long walk. I watch the sunset knowing that the next day will dawn as your BIRTH day.

As the rosy light finally makes way for darkness, your parents and soon-to-be Uncle Avi return. Avi, my 13-year-old son, rushes over to me and whispers, "Did you know, the baby is coming?" Already he is the expert in water breaking and timed contractions. When your Papa Lee arrives home, we sit around the kitchen table eating cookies, laughing, and talking until Betsy, the midwife, calls and orders us to go to sleep. "You are in for the long haul, you must get some rest," she scolds.

Drifting half-awake half asleep, I open my eyes to see your Daddy, my oldest son, Moses, standing at my bedside. He invites me to join them downstairs. I step into a room suffused in the golden glow of candlelight, warmed by the woodstove. Walking in contemplative circles is a beautiful, white-gowned goddess. Do you recognize her? That is your mommy. How can you resist this safe, beckoning arrival point?

> *A time to laugh and a time to weep, turn, turn, turn*

We call your Aunt Elyn, who promises to be over soon. Making tea for everyone, I look around the kitchen and decide to put up a batch of bread. Bringing you down to earth is bound to be hungry work. Papa Lee wakes up wondering what the pounding is all about. I'm just kneading the bread dough. Your Mom is moving around, talking and laughing, she seems so strong and relaxed. Your dad is in total readiness but not sure what to do. "Okay let's get this show on the road," he seems to say.

I think it must be around three in the morning when we call the midwives. We know you are heading this way but cannot tell if you are just around the corner or still far down the road. My breath forms clouds of rising dreams in the cold, clear night as I greet the midwives. Are the tomatoes in danger of freezing when it was so hot just a few days before? There's a change in the wind. I can feel autumn's approach, the time of frost and plants dying. Yet it is filled with the promise of new life. The seeds are formed and saved for spring. This is a time of harvest, a time of new seeds. It is a good time to be born.

A time to plant, a time to reap,
turn, turn, turn

The calm efficiency of the midwives spreads like a prayer through all the corners of the room. Everything is copacetic. After a good dose of loving observation, they suggest once again that we should all try to sleep. Maybe I will lie down for just a bit.

Another dawn begins to sneak its way through the chilly darkness, and as if you too are awakening, the pace quickens. Your mother, with great concentration and grace, keeps working. Elyn sits by her, constantly encouraging her with a touch, a word, a hushed sound, a cooling washcloth.

A time to gain and a time to lose,
turn, turn, turn

By 7 AM, it is time to get you out. Papa Lee comes down dressed for work. "Don't go," I say. "It will be soon, very soon." My brother, Peter, comes with his son Morgan. I rush around trying to figure out what is wrong with the camera. Your mom and dad are hugging on the bed.

A time to build up, a time to tear down
a time to embrace without fear

There is a time to weep and a time to laugh, and this is both. The miracle! What else can we call it? Here is this new life, full of possibility and promise clamoring for that first rosy-colored breath. At long last, a true gift of the god's, you are snuggled against your mom, all 10 pounds and 10 ounces of you—big, beautiful and quiet. We gasp for joy and wonder. It is almost too much to take in. You are here, pink and healthy, ten fingers and ten perfect toes. Joy has filled the room. We rush out to tell the waiting men, who like the magi, file in to see you. Your Uncle Avi cannot take his eyes off you. With a twinkle in his eyes, he places a soccer ball at your feet. You seem so tiny and fragile in comparison. But it is never too early to begin training.

Jyasi, you are the calm amidst all the excited activity. There seems to be little doubt that you intended to come down to earth right now, in this place, to these parents. You make these lovely little chanting sighs like the Tibetan monks whose recorded chants filled the air with peace all morning.

A time for peace, I swear it's not too late

I sit in the rocking chair holding you. This is me, your grandma Mumi, rocking gently. I think—*When he is older, he will come into the garden with me to pick tomatoes. We will bake bread together, and he can put in raisins and cinnamon and as much honey as he wants. I will try to be wise for him, but we will laugh a lot.* And I imagine walking with your hand in mine as we go up the road to see the horse and hunt for frogs in the pond. I imagine...well, *turn, turn, turn, there is a time for that under heaven.*

In peace,
Grandma Mumi

200

Welcome to Rwanda

It still takes a bit of time to fly around the world. Somehow, I expect it to be faster. In one day, we can make it all the way to the other side of the planet. No small miracle. It used to take eighty days to travel around the world and before that, much longer, so I shouldn't complain. But when you are actually squeezed into a 24 by 28-inch space breathing dry, recycled air and eating spongy carbohydrates, practically indistinguishable from the wrappings they are served in, and pretending to sleep, it can seem like a long 26 hours. After a few cat naps, many walks down the aisle to the restroom, a couple of movies, and a few meals, I am soon to land in Kigali, the capital of Rwanda.

On the first leg of this journey, I sat next to a man named Fred. He came from Nairobi but lives in Iowa. What are the chances of meeting an African who is now an American from Iowa? What a story. When he was in high school, he found a book in his village's tiny school library about Martin Luther King. He was so inspired that, then and there, he decided he would one day go visit MLK's birthplace. At the end of high school, he made his way to Ebenezer Baptist Church in Atlanta and, from there he determined to go to college in the USA. While in college, he met a lovely Midwestern preacher's daughter who became his wife. They are now the proud parents of three beautiful little children. I saw the pictures! He loves where he lives, though he laughed when I asked if there are any people of color there. He said his in-laws took it in stride, but his wife's grandmother was a bit stunned at first. He is building a house in his home village outside of Nairobi where his mother lives. He intends to raise his children in both countries. Wow. I might have missed that story if I had stayed home.

One Thousand Hills

Rwanda is the land of one thousand hills—beautiful, green, fertile hills. I was on my way there to teach CRM, the Community Resilience Model, a biologically-based model for working with trauma that is taught by the Trauma Resource Institute. First we were going to teach a group of psychology students. Then we would move on to teach childcare workers, and finally, a group of farmers at a coffee/tea plantation.

Before departing, I immersed myself in the history and culture of Rwanda. This tiny, densely populated, landlocked country in the middle of Africa has a rich yet tumultuous history. Rwanda is the size of Maryland, but where Maryland has a population of 6 million people, Rwanda has 12 million, and its population is rapidly increasing. In fact, almost half the people are under 15-years old. It has a perfect climate with both rainy and dry seasons, and it is wonderfully green. People were quite surprised when I told them that we can only grow food from May to September at home. "How do you get enough to eat?" they want to know. This is where Diane Fossey met her gorillas and where she was later killed. Rwanda was colonized first by the Germans and then handed over to Belgium until it claimed its independence in 1962. Like many countries in Africa, it is still reeling from the debilitating effects of colonialism.

Rwandans are drawn from just one cultural and linguistic group made up of three subgroups: the Hutu,

Tutsi, and Twa. Most of us know something about the horrifying genocide in Rwanda. In 1994, over the course of approximately 100 days, almost 1million Tutsi and thousands of politically moderate Hutu were slaughtered with machetes—men, women, and little children. It was neighbors killing neighbors. The horror was beyond imagination. The rest of the world stood by and did nothing. Bill Clinton said that his inaction in regards to Rwanda was one of the biggest regrets of his presidency. When the RFP government gained control, approximately 2 million Hutu fled to Zaïre, Burundi, and the Congo. For the past twenty years, Rwanda has been attempting to recover using reconciliation and justice work, with the establishment of the International Criminal Tribunal for Rwanda (ICTR) and the reintroduction of *Gacaca*, a traditional village court system.

Paul Kagame, a former freedom fighter and the president of Rwanda since shortly after the genocide, has managed to keep the peace. The government is 98% Tutsi, and ethnic animosity or solidarity is illegal as are public mention of either Tutsi or Hutu ethnicity. All references to ethnic origin have been stricken from official documents. But the people we talked to say it is always known or quickly deduced who your people are. And the animosity has merely slipped just below the surface.

The Twa are forest-dwelling pygmy people descended from Rwanda's earliest inhabitants. They were almost wiped out during the genocide. Recently, those remaining were evicted from their forest homes for conservation and commercial projects and received little or no compensation. They eke out a barely subsistence survival.

203

On this journey, you will find MaryLynn, a brilliant social worker and master trainer in the Trauma Resiliency Model, who is from Asheville. She and I have worked together before. Sara, the youngest of our group, organized and orchestrated this whole trip: trainings, itinerary, hotels, guides, and so much more. She always looked stylish and ready and is reassuringly competent. To complete the fantastic four (in addition to me), there was Lynn, a retired health worker from Asheville with non-stop energy and an ever-ready laugh. We quickly bonded and were ready to work, wander, and laugh together.

In addition, we had an impressive in-country team. Naik'ay, our translator, was a competent young woman, who looked like an Egyptian princess and spoke flawless Kinyawandan, French, and English. Alex, wiry and funny, used almost passable English and is our go-fer. He works at Hotel Rwanda, famous for the movie with Don Cheadle. Lastly, was Jaffe, our quiet, unflappable driver.

Our team from the US would be joined by some in-country partners after we taught them this model. The idea was that they would use it and teach others to use it.

CRM is an effective model of nervous system regulation that can be used in many settings, formal and informal, to reset the nervous system and allow an individual to return to a place of resiliency. It has been brought to many disaster recovery zones in Haiti, China, and the Philippines, taught to active duty military and veterans, Head Start workers and community organizations, and to U.S. shooting survivors to name only a few.

204

I am sorry to say that the need for this kind of skill will probably not be ending anytime soon since. As far as I can tell, there seems to be no end to trauma. But what I especially love about this model is that it does not require an expert or professional. We can teach it and leave it behind for people to use and pass on. We even offered the training to a group of novitiates (soon to be nuns) who were to be placed in rural sites where there are many challenges. They were pleased to have a new tool to use. We always begin each day with a song, and they sang in four-part harmonies, which sounded like angels had come down to encourage us.

One day, we four trainers went to a special Sunday lunch at John Yves. He was the manager of Step Town, the hotel where we were staying. He had a new wife and newer baby, Gabriel, and he invited us for dinner. It seemed like a lot of work and expense, so we asked if he was sure he wanted us all. He said more guests brought more blessings, but I think it was a bit overwhelming. First they shared their wedding album with us. Weddings and graduations are BIG deals, and the pictures were prolific. At last a multi-course meal was set on the table (there was a maid hidden in the kitchen—I peeked). When John Yves wife heard that we do not have help at home she was amazed. "You mean you must work a job and come home to take care of the children and the house?" she asked. "And who cooks for you and does the laundry?" We have to do it ourselves, we told her. She was aghast, and her estimation of the rich USA plummeted at that news.

On to Butare

The stories piled up like fallen leaves in autumn, faster than I could write them. My only free time was a sliver of evening when I needed to go to sleep. I sat under the throne of my mosquito netting writing late into the evening.

One day, we woke early, packed into two cars, and took off for Butare. Once the capital of Rwanda, Butare is a university town and much quieter and less sophisticated than the capital. It was a hair-raising, twisting ride with stunning views of lush terraced hillsides, goats grazing on any available sliver of grass, and people carrying every possible thing on their heads. Motorbikes and bicycles proliferated at every intersection. I watched but never spotted a single woman riding, except on the back.

We pulled into the university campus right on time. We were scheduled to teach a group of psychology students at a four-day Train the Trainer Community Resilience Training. This was our first work here. In typical African fashion, the room was still being cleaned, so we were sent to check in at the hotel first.

Now that sounds pretty simple, right? WRONG! Nothing is simple in Africa. First we had to find the hotel. Then we had to search for where to check in. Then we had to negotiate the price. Passports had to be shown and the registration filled out by the one lady behind the desk. V e r y s l o w l y. There were throngs of people swirling near the check in. We had to push our way back and forth through about 150 people. Turns out, they were nurses, all dressed up, returning from nursing school in Burundi. They were taking a qualifying test so that they can be hired here in Rwanda. Jobs were scarce everywhere, but still more likely here.

At last, we returned to the teaching site, and our students were waiting. They had been there since early morning. Very young, all dressed up, and exceedingly well-groomed, the twenty-six students, half men and half women, looked towards us in polite expectation. We scurried to set up our Powerpoint. I don't even want to tell you how long that took. Many plugs, computers, and attempts later, we figured it out, only to watch as all the power blinked off. But we are nothing if not intrepid, and we eventually continued without props.

As soon as we began the introductions, we hit the language barrier hard. We had been assured that these students spoke English and that a translator was not necessary. All of Rwanda schools are now officially English-speaking. About six years before, after speaking French as their second language for decades, President Kagame decreed that all students, from 1st grade through college, must be taught in English. Many of the teachers could barely speak or understand English, let alone teach it, but if they admitted that, they would lose their jobs. So officially, they all spoke English.

Well big surprise, official and actual may not always be identical. We asked them to share their name, where their names came from, and something that makes them happy. We understood very little. It was terrible to tell someone who thinks they are speaking English that you cannot understand them. Some of it was the pronunciation, some was the syllable emphasis, and some simply the lack of proficiency. And I have heard mice that speak louder than these girls. It seems that in Rwanda, girls are supposed to be unseen and unheard.

Niak'ay, our translator, had already performed miracles translating our now unused slides and now she stepped up to help. We plowed on, but trying to find teaching examples and metaphors that these students could relate to was a challenge. At one point, I used traveling in an airplane to describe something. What was wrong with me? Not one of them had ever been on an airplane. The biggest hit of the day might have been when I dragged around the room being sad and then skipped around being happy in a slapstick attempt to explain our nervous system. They got the difference!

We also learned that you cannot ask for volunteers to answer questions because there will be none. It is considered rude to put yourself forward like a know-it-all. No one raised a hand ever. We had to remember to call on a student every time. It was a lot for us to learn, but this receptive group made it satisfying. We sent them off with some homework and said we would continue in the morning. Most of them went home to no running water and erratic electricity, and yet, they appeared each morning perfectly cleaned, impeccably dressed, and on time.

We came to admire our group of determined, generous students. The language remained a challenge. Our Kinyarwandan was limited to *hello* and *how are you*. Most of the students struggled to express themselves in English. However, by the end, they were practicing the skills in small groups in a mix of Kinyarwandan and English, and it seemed to work. Their enthusiasm was boundless. By the end, they talked of bringing these new skills everywhere—to children, alcoholics, families, and genocide survivors.

These young people were the best and the brightest in the country. They had to pass difficult exams to be admitted to school, and most had high hopes for improving the well-being of people in their country. I spoke to Evangeline, a serious, shy, young man who hoped to go back to his village and help people there. Another student, Sam, had just graduated and was already working with mental health, a topic that had only recently been introduced there. Alcohol abuse and domestic violence were epidemic, and the generational after-effects of genocide can barely be imagined. Mental health work is so new, in fact, that we learned the names of all six psychologists in the country. Unfortunately, unemployment was exceedingly high and whether they will actually get a job after graduation was doubtful.

We ended our four-day training in Butare with a ceremonial commencement complete with a procession, handshakes, graduation certificates, and multiple group photos followed by a tearful goodbye.

Drop A Key

First thing in the morning, we bade goodbye to Butare and set out for Gisenyi where we would be offering a one day workshop to fifty workers at a coffee and tea cooperative on Kivu Lake near the Congo. This is a place both poor and difficult to reach, and visitors were a rare event. The trip took all day along winding roads swarming with people who carried bananas, roof tiles, and farming tools on their heads. And, of course, let's not forget the babies wrapped tightly on their backs. I love that swaddling! Much of the green land was covered in cabbage, potatoes, and assorted crops and corn hung to dry from the eaves. I didn't see any tractors or beasts of burden, only saw bicycles and motorbikes.

After travelling all morning, we stopped at a tiny, rudimentary town to find a bathroom and get a drink. A woman led Sara and I to the bathroom. It was a rickety, tiny goat stall. This was about as rough as it got. Outside in the dirt would have been better. Sara went first while I waited holding our bags. Sara, our competent guide had managed all the complicated plans thus far, but she emerged from the dark structure pale and shaking. "Something awful just happened," she gasped grabbing my hands. *Oh no, I think, what could it be—a snake bite, an illness? Here we are as far from civilization as we can get. Not something terrible!*

She finally confessed that the car keys had fallen out of her pocket and down the latrine hole. Oh my God! Those latrines were so dark and deep. People actually fell in and died in them every year. How would we ever retrieve the key?

Our car was locked on the side of the road, and the keys were down in the hole. We took a breath. I reminded us both that we were okay, no one was injured, and there had been no snake bites. We would figure this out somehow.

In a very few minutes, people began to gather around us. They sensed something was up. Niak'ay quickly sent all the white women into the tiny soda shop that had nothing to sell to get us out of sight. Then she and Jofay got to work. Pretty soon, there was an expanding fraternity of men all bent over the car. While they were working on it, an energized group of teenage boys gathered at the latrine. Their excitement was building. What were they doing? Someone came running with a long stick which they tied with a rag to two additional sticks. We suspected they were about to go fishing, but clearly not the ordinary kind.

It might have been all of thirty-five minutes

before the men had successfully broken into the car, taken the key cylinder out, and replaced it with one that must be turned on with a screwdriver. It wasn't ideal, but it was functioning, and that may be the power of Africa!

Things were almost settled, and we were getting ready to drive off when the mob of boys came running up from the latrine cheering and triumphantly waving the keys, which they had kindly washed! Of course, by that time, we could no longer use the keys, but it was no use explaining that to this enthusiastic crowd. Instead there followed a major haggling session. The small cash reward was settled on, and we were once more on the road. The whole thing probably took less than an hour. Africa is such a wonder; the people are exceedingly self-reliant.

We had a new saying after that. When anyone needed to go to the bathroom, we said, "I think I have to go drop a key."

COOPAC Coffee Growers

Next was the Kivu coffee and tea cooperative, a place of poor Hutu farm workers—Hutu because there were no Tutsi survivors in this area. Many of the men from here were still in prison. We saw some prison work gangs, dressed in either pink or orange, on the road. The orange ones had confessed their deeds, told survivors where their loved-ones bodies might be found, and asked the relatives for forgiveness. They served a shorter sentence than the ones in pink, who had not confessed.

To address the fact that there were thousands of accused still awaiting trial in the national court system, and to bring about justice and reconciliation at the grassroots level, the Rwandan government, in 2005, re-established the traditional community court system called "Gacaca" (pronounced GA-CHA-CHA).

In the Gacaca system, communities at the local level elected judges to hear the trials of genocide suspects accused of crimes. The courts gave lower sentences if the person confessed, was repentant, and sought reconciliation with the community. Often, confessing prisoners returned home without further penalty or received community service orders. More than 12,000 community-based courts tried more than 1 million cases throughout the country.

The Gacaca trials also served to promote reconciliation by providing a means for victims to learn the truth about the death of their family members. They gave perpetrators the opportunity to confess their crimes, show remorse, and ask for forgiveness in front of their communities and sometimes even show where the bodies could be found. This was a small country, and the prisoners often returned to live side by side with the families of their victims.

We drove up the road to the farm. What a road it was. I would label it a dirt crater at best—winding, deeply rutted, and almost completely washed out in places. Sometimes we had to get out and walk. Other times, the car had to back up and try again. Slowly, we edged further up, passing people and children as they waved from their tiny villages. But always the gorgeous Kivu Lake, shining silver, dotted with fishing boats, and soaring birds, spread out beneath us.

There was very little land left fallow or scrub growth here. All had been put to use, terraced, and populated. The people dressed in rags and many were hungry. After almost an hour and maybe ten miles, we came to a stop. Here we could take only the bigger car, which meant two trips.

In addition to our teaching team, we were joined for the day by three specially chosen students who had just completed the training at the University two days before. There was Sam, a sweet young man, who loved Manchester United with an unparalleled enthusiasm and wrote three senior dissertations all in English, and Evariste, a quiet, older man (maybe 35) who was married with two children. He was from this area, so he was deeply pleased to be selected. And lastly, there was Ernest who requires a whole book for himself. Skinny as a tree branch, he dressed in a tangerine orange sports jacket that he had made, illustrated everything in elaborate pencil sketches, and shared laughter yoga with us all.

At last, after climbing the last few hundred feet up steep terrain, we entered a cinder block classroom where the chosen participants sat three to a bench. They had been waiting for us since 8:30 AM. It was now around 10 AM.

The row by the window was all men. The middle row mixed men in the front and women in the back, and the third row was all women. They were dressed in their best—a mishmash of African, American, and Indian clothing. The women look regal and ready. The men looked reserved and skeptical.

We offered some welcoming words and asked them if they would stand up and share a song. The women began and soon were clapping and dancing. The oldest women moved with the most enthusiasm. Then they went around and said their names, their work, and something that made them happy. It took a while, but this was important. Some were happy with their

213

religion, one was happy with money, and many were happy that we had come.

After all the introductions, we taught the concepts of the model. But rather than the cumbersome, slow process of speaking and being translated, we very quickly turned it over to our graduates. They took over with a passion, teaching and telling stories and acting everything out. Before our wide eyes, the model was sprouting wings and taking flight! The people nodded, commented, and were totally engaged. And we merely served as coaches to our graduates.

When we got to the tracking, where people learn to notice what is happening inside their bodies and begin to practice paying attention to places of greater comfort, we asked Ernest to lead everyone in laughter yoga. I invited in the children who were all peeking in at the open door and glass-free windows to come stand in front. They all looked so serious until Ernest got them going. Soon everyone was shaking in big, belly-shaking laughter. Then we asked them to notice what was happening inside. We watched as the room changed from worn-down skeptics to joyful participants. They got it!

We broke for lunch not knowing how and when it would arrive on this barebones mountaintop, but soon a couple of women and men appeared carrying three huge pots of beans and rice. They served us first, then the men, then the women. After the adults had eaten, they gave what was left to the patient and hungry children.

When we came back to practice, they brought up the example of a husband and wife fighting. It turned out that in the front row to my left was a husband who was a leader of COOPAC, the coffee cooperative. In the front row to the right was his wife. She started the day looking very sour and uninvolved, and she had said that she could not be happy. But after our time together, she proclaimed that she loved her husband and went to him with a big hug. The whole room erupted in applause! I was not quite sure what happened, but whatever it was, it worked.

We ended with "He's Got the Whole World in his Hands." Then we all joined in a song and dance they taught us. In the end, we linked hands in a big circle and asked each person to offer one word. Finally, of course, we all go out for the group photo shoot.

But the Best Part of this Story is the P.S.!

P.S.: The next day, Sara went to tour the coffee farms where she met a few people who were at the training. One very old man told her that he walked forty miles round trip to get there. They expressed how much the training had meant to them and that they were using it to stay in their resilient zone! The little gentleman said that his house was now a happier place.

A Short Fish Tale

It all started with a seemingly simple invitation: "Why don't you come with us to British Columbia to fly fish?"

Fly fish? Isn't that something rich, blond men (think Robert Redford) do in between golf and sailing? But Paradise Lake beckoned, and I'm no fool; when paradise calls, I go.

My husband's cousin George is an outdoor freak. He lives to do anything— fish, sail, hike, climb, bike, kayak—as long as he is outside, preferably somewhere stunningly beautiful. We met him in Seattle and then drove due north into the middle of nowhere. We passed thousands upon thousands of uninterrupted firs standing rigidly at attention before China-blue teacup lakes spilled carelessly into their midst. Except for a few log cabins, humans did not seem to belong here.

We found our cabin and got down to the business of paradise. Before we had unpacked, George offered instruction and practice. The fly must be cast using a fly rod, reel, and a specialized weighted line. Casting a nearly weightless fly or lure requires well-honed techniques. In the forward cast, the angler whisks the fly into the air back over the shoulder until the line is nearly straight. Then you must cast forward using primarily the forearm. The objective of this motion is to bend the rod tip with stored energy, then transmit that energy to the line. With a mix of skill and luck this would result in the line and the attached fly soaring out for an appreciable distance.

I woke up in the morning from a dream in which I had been instructing myself on the proper form of fly fishing: elbow to your side, upper arm hinged, do not flick your wrist, let the line unfurl in a graceful arc. Rather like a cowboy about to rope a steer. Over and over again, I repeated this motion. I was already exhausted, and the day was just beginning.

Before long, I found myself sitting in a royal blue blow-up seat, which is a hybrid cross between a bumper car and a floating playpen. After donning myriad layers of fleece and micro fibers topped by jolly green suspender pants, I stuffed my sock-covered feet into large boots and even larger flippers. Then, I dropped backwards onto my indigo float, as walking was then out of the question. I arranged myself upright, buoyantly perched upon the water, with my bent legs ready to propel me backwards around the lake.

Attempting to master the precarious navigation skills needed, I almost dropped my $1,000 rod, which I had already insulted by calling a fishing pole. I lunged for the pole, I mean rod, as it is rolled into the brink and caught my palm on the hook, I mean lure. The lure is a Brian Chen, a tiny turquoise sparkly thing that looks a lot like a craft-fair earring, except it has lost its mate and gained a hook.

There I sat in the middle of the breathtakingly beautiful lake ready to begin. *After the flick, let it soar*, I told myself, *straight out, follow it with your eye, your arm, your intention*. The bait should land in a straight line, not those loop de loops that stretch out a good thirty feet in front. Now keep in mind, this was all accomplished while I was paddling, steering, and trying in vain to keep the drunken hook from knotting itself around the pole part of my fishing rod.

So, I figured that was it: cast, swish-swish, swish, swish-flump. I thought, *Yeehaw, cowboy, you're getting the hang of it!* Only, I quickly discovered you shouldn't whoop and slap the side of the floatation chair in exultation. Remember the fish? It seems trout do not like expressions of enthusiasm and consequently will swim away. Oh well, in the oh-so-picky world of fly fishing, this was just the beginning.

I learned that if I counted slowly while allowing the hook to sink one foot for each number and left it exactly level with the trout's pouty little mouths, with any luck, they would swallow the Brian Chen lure. Next, I figured I should act like a bug. The fact that there are no Brian Chen bugs did not deter me. I simply would act as if I were a Brian Chen bug. I pulled in the chartreuse line. The fish, who were gaining a reputation as the brightest being on the planet, may overlook this. That is, they'd overlook it if I kept the line loop-free, low, and far from where they shop for dinner. I saw one fish inspecting the sparkly Brian Chen insect on its invisible few feet of liter. My subtle wrist movements were causing it to slither, twist, and turn just like the bug I had imagined it to be.

This fooled our hungry hero who proceeded to give it a test bump. Imagine that exasperating kid on the playground, the one with the perpetually slobbering nose, who with barely a hint of provocation, lowers his head and charges blindly into any group of two or more happily playing children. He should be sent to juvie for wielding a dangerous weapon, but is instead taken aside by a tired mother who pats him distractedly and sends him off in the other direction.

I was bumped and was paying close attention. My form was correct, my lure was sparkling, the lake was serene, my motorboat legs were paddling, and I was ready to catch that fish. Nothing happened. And I mean nothing. Not a bump, not a ripple, not an insect. What's going on down there? Someone must have sounded a clarion call—A*ll fish below deck!*

After an hour or so of this gripping drama, I looked behind me and saw that I had been blown clear across the lake and was about to crash land on shore. I needed a quick come-about. But there was no steering wheel, no rudder, and no way on earth I could make my huge, fin-like appendages turn this boat around.

Twenty minutes later, sweat dripping into my multiple layers, I was panting like a Golden Retriever. But I had turned one hundred and eighty degrees and had made it back to center. Add navigational abilities to my list of recent accomplishments, though I risked a look around hoping no one had seen this fiasco.

With all the excitement, another half hour passed. I threw all technique to the wind, and that was when I got a giant bump on the line. Holy Jumping Jehoshaphat! This fellow was not just knocking, he was trying to steal my sparkly blue Brian Chen, and he was pulling me with him. *Hang on! Here we go! Think girl, think.* In case of a bite, *oh yeah, strip.* Though it was tempting to get into a rhinestone-encrusted thong to match my Brian Chen, this was not the time for it! I raised the rod triumphantly and started to pull the bright line down into my boat. Whoever that was at the end of my line was now coming towards me at a frightening speed. But mid-rush, he suddenly decided the disco was in the other direction and did an about face. It was obvious who was in control here. We did the do-si-do—him pulling and rushing and me pulling and reeling—until we were finally face to face. Have you ever been face to face with a trout? He was all dolled up in rainbow sparkles. His mouth was moving, and I was sure he must have known the secret of the universe. Unfortunately I couldn't quite hear him. After a short moment, he started to flop, something he did not seem all that pleased about. We couldn't go on this way. It was a cross-species relationship doomed before it had barely begun. "The net! The net," someone from shore screamed. I groped behind me and found a minuscule net into which I was supposed to place this huge (well alright, twelve-incher, but this is, after all, a fish tale) flopping, spinning trout. Yeah right.

Let me assure you, I did indeed land the pretty fellow. I somehow removed the hook, admired his beauty, and then triumphantly held him out above the water to sing him on his way. "Go free!" I exclaimed as I let him go. I could only imagine the tall human tales that would circulate around the swaying seaweed tonight.

At that point, I became desperately aware of my need for a pit stop. If you can picture how hard it was to get into this float and dressed in my layers of clothes, you still cannot begin to imagine the almost insurmountable challenge of doing it all in reverse while keeping your legs tightly crossed and dancing up and down in place. I will spare you the lurid details. Suffice it to say, I am now an experienced fly fisherwoman, and anyone who doubts it is asking for a fight. I challenge all comers to a casting competition. The first one to hook a tree or any other stationary object wins!

Kitty of My Dreams

The waves were as high as a three-story building, and they threatened to swamp the small ship. It was creaking as if the mast was about to snap in two. There was water everywhere; slashing rain, splashing waves, and tears all mingling together. And then... I floundered into consciousness. It was the middle of a dark night with a gentle rain drumming on our tin roof, and the only light came from the green 2:38 on my clock. But the squeaking continued. If it was not the mast of my proverbial pirate ship, what was it? As I lay listening, I finally identified it as a cat's desperate meowing. I tried to go back to sleep, but the sound and my questions began to merge together. *Whose cat could it be? Is it caught in a trap? Could it have been attacked by raccoons?* At last, giving up on a sleep that was not to be, I crept down the stairs, slipped my rubber garden boots on under my white nightgown, and stood in my front yard listening. There it was, sharp and desperate. The unmistakable cry was coming from the cornfield.

In August, the corn really is as high as the elephant's eye. I plunged in and was quickly swallowed by the endless rows. They slapped me from knees to scalp until I was dripping in unity with each tasseled green giant. I followed the feline call. After walking along the rows, I stopped to listen and then headed off in a new direction. This went on for quite some time before it dawned on me—*I am going in circles. I am in a corn maze, in the middle of the night, soaking wet, and someone or something with a sense of humor is leading me on a wild goose chase.* That was when I decided to

221

return to bed, although sleep remained as elusive as that mysterious feline.

Later that morning, I placed a small bowl of cat food just inside the cornfield. Nothing. The next day, I brought it a few feet into our yard and watched and waited on my porch. I was finally rewarded with a glimpse of a ball of grey fluff, but it scurried back into the cornfield at my approach. I was not going back to cornfield pursuits. It took me two more days of moving the food ever closer until I lured him right onto the porch. As he fearfully approached, I pounced. Grasped firmly in my two hands, the little guy panicked, but then he seemed to breathe a sigh of relief as his body went limp.

He was the size of an overweight Beanie Baby and couldn't have been 6 weeks old. My family and I figured he was dumped in the country field by someone who couldn't keep him. A few days later, we found his much quieter, less dramatic brother perched on the volleyball post in our front yard. We named them Romulus and Remus, after the twin sons of the priestess Rhea who was fathered by Mars, the god of war. Like their namesakes, ours also started out as feral babies and became the founders not of Rome but of our humble home.

We are a family of cat people, but we were in between cats, having lost our elder statesman not long before these two made themselves right at home. Romulus turned out to be as determined in his loving family involvement as he was in his original elusiveness, and Remus went on to perch and fall off many high places.

It has been awhile since I twirled ghostlike and slightly mad through cornfields covered in wet pollen,

222

but on those hazy summer nights when I can't sleep, I find myself listening, or am I dreaming once again?

Nagel All-but-the-Kitchen-Sink Lunch

Here's our fallback, always welcome lunch. It is perfect for anytime. Like when anyone drops in for lunch needing a little pick-me-up or even after a long night in the cornfields. I thought everyone ate lunch this way until we had some people over who were clearly stymied by this grab and build your own commotion. The first thing you need to eliminate is any desire for neatness. The next to go is silverware and, finally, shyness. This is a pile-it-on, drip-a-little, and go-for-it meal. Satisfying and communal, you will find that it encourages fascinating conversation and comradery.

Likely and Possible Ingredients

The amounts vary depending on the number of hungry mouths and availability of items.

- Bread or bagels– fresh and local recommended
- Red onion
- Avocado
- Lettuce and sprouts
- Tomatoes
- Sauerkraut
- Hard boiled eggs
- Artichoke hearts
- Pickles
- Banana peppers
- Roasted red peppers
- Hummus
- Mayonnaise, mustard, pesto
- Cheeses of various kinds
- Tapenade

We display everything that can be found on big boards, baskets, and bowls, sliced and diced and spread out across the table or counter. Everyone helps themselves. Ready, set, make your own sandwich! The type is limited only by what's there and how much you can pile on. Of course, later you will face the challenge of getting it from plate into mouth, but there you are on your own.

Woodchuck Sighting

It was still bone-chillingly cold, the ground and driveway both covered with ice and snow. Yet on one little patch of old grass, there he sat looking like the ruler of the kingdom.

A woodchuck has very few endearing qualities. Though he is four-legged and furry, he is really a hairy, muscled bullet, a round, mean, eating machine, kind of like a storage tube with teeth. He does not pick and choose and say, "A leaf for me, a leaf for you." No, he strolls into the garden and eats his way from one end to the other, leaving nothing in his wake but a few bare, stubby stems.

Think of children's books with animal characters. *Winnie the Pooh, Wind in the Willows:* no woodchuck— a badger, yes, rat, sure but not even Kenneth Grahame could make a woodchuck look cute. They tried it in *Groundhog Day* (yes, a groundhog is a woodchuck), but they had Bill Murray, so sure.

Woodchucks have sharp teeth, long claws, and are known for their aggression. You do not want to come face to face with one of them in a tight space. They move 5,500 pounds of earth for each burrow, creating 46 feet of tunnel that can undermine trees and foundations. Through these tunnels, they prowl under our feet, and we have no idea.

This garden annihilation machine was perched barely 10 feet outside my window. And I knew: where there is one, there are dozens. I couldn't discern much beyond big, small, and the one with the contemptuous smile, but they must have established an extended clan by now. These guys had been moving in on us, getting closer every year since our dog grew old and weary. They peppered our land with gigantic craters and took over our crumbling shed, which is a McMansion for the furry foes. Burrowed under the shed, they now ambled along their extended territory with nary a witness.

We had tried everything to deter them. First, we filled in their holes. Hah! Then we fenced in some of the gardens. That showed them for a while until they figured out how to dig under and climb over. After all, our fresh broccoli and chard was being grown just for them, wasn't it? We tried Have-a-Heart traps. These guys are very wily. Why come in the trap for kale when they could pick it fresh? We caught a couple of piss-angry raccoons and one very chill skunk, but no woodchucks.

Now the time had come—vegetarianism and peaceable nation be damned! We had a gun. OK, it was really just a step up from a toy. It took these little bullets; well, I do not think they are even called bullets. They were pellets smaller than my last pimple and probably only as annoying to the woodchuck as that pimple was to me. Target practice came first. We are a family who vehemently eschewed firearms. I regularly ranted about the importance of gun control. But there I was in the field with a big mama rifle slung over my shoulder. I practiced with a 6x8 piece of plywood. Bam! I hit it. That wasn't too hard. Then we drew a circle on the board. That required a bit more skill. I moved on to tin cans. Ka-pow! Shooting straight was a satisfying accomplishment, though my gun was too rinky-dink to create enough force to knock the tin can over. And I was trying to picture how I would graduate from aiming at tin cans to aiming at a breathing creature, one with eyes and a heart. I was not sure I could do it.

Of course, even if I overcame that hurdle—I was desperate after all—they were so suspicious. Woodchucks do not easily let you get close enough to shoot. By the time I loaded, cocked, aimed, and fired, they would be long gone, chuckling as they sauntered away.

Don't make the mistake of thinking you have ONE woodchuck in your yard. There are more of these beasts now then there were when the European settlers first stepped out of their ocean vessels. They reproduce in thirty-two days. Thirty-two! I can't even clean my house that often. That is less time than it takes me to grow a crop of kale. Civilization is not hurting them, and I was clearly not hurting them either. They are so far off the endangered species list that there is little doubt that they will be here long after our species is gone. Though I do wonder who will raise the salad greens for them. By killing off all their predators— wolves, coyotes, and foxes—we have given them a carte blanche.

You know what gets me more than anything? Woodchucks can climb trees. I never imagined that those stubby legs and clumsy bodies could climb a tree. I might as well surrender. They have probably posted a sentry up in a tree beside my house, and he sits there picking his teeth and watching me.

With a piercing whistle (yes they whistle as warning), I was sure he was telling others that I was on my way outside. No wonder they knew when I was coming. I was not going to be making woodchuck stew anytime soon.

I can think of one positive outcome connected to woodchucks. I have had conversations with neighbors, workmen, and various passerbys about (drum roll) the woodchuck solution, including, but not limited to, the best firearms to use. It turns out that everyone has an opinion, a suggestion, or an experience to share. Meanwhile the tunnels keep increasing and my crops continue to be devoured. It might be time for a *Chicken Soup for the Woodchuck Soul* publication. Send your best entries to me.

From Pete Seeger to Caffe Lena

Pete Seeger is gone! It sure seemed like he would always be here. After almost a century, how could he leave now? We need him. Will the world be able to keep spinning without him? You name a good cause, and he was on it. I think he had something to do with keeping our poor ole world on track. Without him, the rest of us are going to have to step up.

I am not quite old enough to go all the way back to Pete Seeger's first performances with Woody Guthrie, which began in the 1940's, or back to the Almanac Singers, but I was a dedicated Weavers fan in the late '50s. I had all their albums and could probably sing most of their songs by heart. They ended every concert with "Goodnight, Irene," which I always thought was written for my Aunt Irene. She seemed to have been shaped from the same cloth; they both marched with Martin Luther King in Selma and dedicated their lives to working for justice. I have a vivid memory of going to see the Weavers in concert. I was a small town 10-year old at a big concert, which was rare in those days. The huge hall was filled with thousands of people (well, OK, maybe hundreds). There they were on stage—Pete Seeger, Fred Hellerman, Lee Hays, and Ronnie Gilbert. I remember, "Wimoweh, wimoweh, in the jungle, the mighty jungle, the lion sleeps tonight" and "Kisses Sweeter Than Wine" and, of course, "Goodnight, Irene."

What was even more amazing, my parents took me backstage that night. It turned out that Ronnie Gilbert was married to Martin Weg, and Marty went to dental school with my daddy. That's only a few degrees of separation, right? As a dedicated Weavers groupie, I marched right backstage like I was important. Gazing up at Ronnie Gilbert—uh-oh, let me stop here and admit—this is supposed to be about Pete Seeger, and I assure you, it is. But, at that time, my awe was reserved for Ronnie Gilbert. She was beautiful in a bright pink, crinoline dress, and she was bending down to talk to me. Completely tongue-tied, I thrust my program in her face for an autograph. Pete once said that Ronnie had a big voice. She could out-sing him standing two feet away from the mike while he was two inches away. And there we were backstage, right beside her!

But back to Pete. Did you know that he was called up to the House on Un-American Activities in 1955? He pleaded the First Amendment stating that it was against his rights as an American to be questioned in this manner. In 1961, he was finally convicted and served a few hours in jail before his conviction was overturned. But for many years, he was banned from performing on radio and TV, and his career, like many others who were blacklisted, tanked.

My friend Al McKinney, who worked with Pete and his wife Toshi on the Clearwater Festival every year, told me that when Pete was asked to talk about those days, he often hesitated. "He doesn't want to talk about yesterday. He wants to figure out how to make today better."

Pete loved to draw. During his family concerts, he sometimes brought an easel up on stage. When Moses was 8 or so, he was picked to climb up on stage and help Pete draw. Moses was already playing cello and a little guitar, and he was quite starstruck. Twenty-five years later, after moving to Beacon with his own family, Moses drove to Pete's very private, off-the-grid house to pick up the paperwork for the Green Party Secretary, a job Pete had been doing since the party's beginning.

Pete Seeger was an inspiration, a wise teacher, a father figure to so many, but Caffe Lena was like my big sister. We grew up together. The Caffe was started in 1960 when I was 10, but it matured a lot faster than I did. (It's not the only one!) My mom and dad hung out there first, attending many shows, and often helping out the owner Lena Spencer as she struggled to pay bills. Dad would sometimes drive down to the bus station an hour away to pick up performers arriving from Boston, New York City, or points west. In those days, one artist performed all weekend and sometimes they slept at our house. Mom and Dad were there when Lena chastised the audience for not listening to a young upstart. "You are going to be hearing more of this young man." My mom and dad left unimpressed by Bob Dylan. "He can't really sing," they said.

As I headed into my teen years and The Beatles had their way with me, I was drawn in. Caffe Lena was where the odd (cool) kids in my school hung out. They were the artists, the beatniks, the pot smokers (though I knew NOTHING of that). It was dark and mysterious, and in those days, very smoky. Lena sat by the stairs with her cat and Dorothea Brownell playing Scrabble, and she occasionally acknowledged one or the other of us youngsters.

At fourteen, *Freewheelin'* was my coming-of-age album. I can still sing you every line of "The Times They are a-Changin."

Come gather round people
Wherever you roam

232

And admit that the waters
Around you have grown
And accept it that soon
You'll be drenched to the bone
If your time to you is worth savin'
Then you better start swimmin'
Or you'll sink like a stone
For the times they are a-changin'

Something seemed to open in me with that music—I wanted to to be part of the terrible, beautiful world. I wanted to live a life that mattered.

Fifteen years later, when Lee and I returned to Saratoga with a child, we became regulars at the Caffe. We were there to hear Rosalie Sorrels sing, "If I Could Be the Rain" and then help her cook her famous lasagna for Lena's birthday. We listened to Dave Van Ronk, who taught Dylan everything he knew, sing wisecracking blues with his trademark scratchy voice and fast-picking fingers. We watched sweet Bill Staines spin tales about opossum-humming and "The Roseville Fair." Moses acted in many of Lena's Christmas productions, though she always called him Noah. Through it all, Lena Spencer was always there.

One evening in 1989, Lena was preparing to go to Albany to attend an opening of the movie *Ironweed*. She had a small part in it and was so excited. Already in poor health, she fell down the steep stairs of the Caffe and passed away a few days later. The Caffe then became a non-profit and struggled to survive. A few years later, I became the President of the board of directors. At that time, when its survival was tenuous at best, we managed to buy the building, hire Sarah Craig and get the Caffe to run in the black for the first time ever!

One autumn, we brought in a new talent—someone tattooed, pierced, and I thought, unknown. However, the young students at Skidmore went nuts over her. Her name was Ani DiFranco. At the last minute, I had to introduce her because she would not let Al McKinney do it. At that time, she wanted to have nothing to do with M-E-N. The main thing I remember about that concert was my shock at her generous sprinkling of the F-word throughout her stage patter. I had brought my young children to the performance and regretted it. That was when that word still had the ability to shock.

So when a dynamic, young woman named Jocelyn Arem showed up, asking lots of questions, we made a connection that is still going strong. She was a junior at Skidmore, an engaged, gentle, singer songwriter who had this curious idea to write her senior thesis about the history of Caffe Lena. Skidmore even created a special major for her. Her questions took her around the country interviewing almost every living person who had ever performed at the Caffe. She went on to a master's degree in Music ethnography and continued working on that mammoth project. A wonderful book, *Caffe Lena: Inside America's Legendary Folk Music Coffeehouse,* eventually came into existence. Check it out!! It is a work of beauty filled with great stories and stunning photographs of the history that happened right here in Saratoga Springs.

You can join me at Caffe Lena for the next concert. You really can't go wrong enjoying folk, roots, blues, jazz, bluegrass, or you name it. Come on through those swinging doors and climb the stairs. I'll meet you there.

Top: House Fire 2001
Bottom: Zimbabwe composting toilet 2006

235

Top: *Walter the Woodchuck*
Bottom: *Caffe Lena 1982*

SEEDS

Family Moth

A story is like water that you heat for your bath.
It takes messages between the fire and your skin.
It lets them meet, and it cleans you!
Rumi

The Nagel family is not shy. We are annoying, perhaps, loud, for sure, pushy, maybe, but not shy. We do not, as a rule, hang back waiting for someone else to take the lead. After becoming a Nagel in the previous century, I already knew this. We have actors and dancers, pianists, oboists and cellists, and even a few engineers. Among us are some community organizers and a couple of clowns, but wallflowers are alien beings for this clan. Most of them embrace a party like it is a long-lost relative. They can be counted on to be the first on the dance floor busting moves that could have come out of *Dancing with the Stars*. At one bar mitzvah, my not-so-young sister-in-law hijacked the band for her personal song and dance interpretation of "Hit Me with Your Best Shot." At 3-years old, my son stood up in a cowboy hat and plastic fringed vest and sang "Oklahoma" for his grandparents' entire gathering of well-dressed guests. So I should not have been surprised that the Nagel family jumped at the chance to do a homemade version of The Moth radio show.

You must have heard of The Moth by now. It was started in 1997 by novelist George Dawes Green as homage to those hot summer nights in Georgia when people gathered on the porch to share stories. On those nights, moths flapped against the screens. In recent years, the show has grown steadily in popularity as people from all walks of life get up on stage to tell their

238

stories. The guidelines are these: the story must be true, it must have happened to the one telling, and it must be told without notes. Usually there is a time limit. Though when it comes to this family, brevity is probably not our strength! With those guidelines, we began.

My college-aged nephew, Ian, is a delightful mix of brash braggadocio and sweet imp. He is from Boulder and recently moved to Montana to attend college. He is doing this at his own pace, which allows him plenty of time for his real passions—skiing and trucks. He can turn amazing 360 degree flips on skis and finds a way to go where no one else has gone. He is happiest when he is on the move.

Ian: *Yeah, so it was almost the weekend. I figure Friday is close enough. Time to get away from school and onto the slopes. A couple of my buddies were ready to go, and, of course, I am always ready to go. So, we grabbed our skis and headed out. Perfect snow—deep and cold. We like to go off-trail, naturally, away from the inexperienced skiers, where there is nothing but white slopes as far as the eye can see. My friend Zach asked if he could come too. Sure, I said. He didn't have any backcountry experience, but I knew I could show him the ropes.*

Jill is my husband's middle sister. She is nothing if not thorough and organized. She manages her family with the same efficiency that she runs the family business with her husband John. I've always been impressed by how she can look so good and arrange a delicious multi-course meal for thirty like it's as easy as

239

throwing in a load of laundry. She likes having her ducks in a row. No loosey goosey here.

Jill: *Many years ago, when John and I had two little children and were expecting our third, we decided to make the move from Connecticut to Colorado. John was recently unemployed, and we didn't know how we were going to survive. But we were determined to head west and take our chances. We sold our house and most of our things, packed up what was left, and set off. The plan was that John would drive the car, pulling the trailer, and I would go ahead by plane with Isabel and Ian, who were 6 and 3. My sister Jody, who lived in Boulder, would pick us up. I had already rented an apartment, sight unseen through a real estate agent.*

Now in her 30s, Kiara is a strong and competent consultant who travels around the world and knows people in cities of every state. She seems to own the stage as soon as she steps up to tell her story. Her thick, dark hair is pulled tightly back. She strides back and forth as she speaks. But when she begins this story, she suddenly becomes that little lost girl again.

Kiara: *Imagine me, if you will, as an innocent child, just turning 6, full of curiosity but new to the ways of the world. My family was staying at a cottage on Cape Cod. It was not much: small, dingy, and filled with plastic furniture. But there was a short, scruffy path to the glorious beach. And even back then, I did love me a good beach. One afternoon, I was impatient with waiting and told my parents that I was going to walk to the beach by myself. I was, after all, a big sister. They reminded me to*

240

stay on the path and not go into the water and said they would be along soon.

I skipped proudly down the path, independence making me feel tall. After all, I was going to be six in a few days. Entranced by the bees, flowers, and pinecones, it wasn't long before that simple path to the beach turned into a labyrinth, and I found myself utterly lost.

The stories roll along like marbles down an incline. Once they gain some momentum, they are unstoppable. Everyone listens, though not all quietly. As an opinionated bunch, you can imagine the raucous comments from the audience. After all, people remember the past differently and want to share their memory as the definitive one. But the person who's up "owns" the stage, and it is their story to tell.

So what is it about storytelling? Why is it such powerful stuff? Joan Didion says, "We tell ourselves stories in order to live." It is that basic, that crucial. I think stories are how we make meaning of life. And without meaning, life is not worth living.

Stories are all around us too—in newspapers, on blogs, on Instagram, on the street corners, and in our homes. People have been telling stories since the beginning of womankind, as those cave drawings prove. Stories move us; they make us feel alive and connected. And, often, they inspire us. Our longing for stories reflects a basic human need to not only understand but to share life. They give us a way to reach out to others.

In fact, research suggests that the more listeners understand the story, the more their brain activity synchs with the storyteller's. This is because when we listen to stories and understand them, we actually experience the same brain pattern as the person telling the story. So by telling a story, we can transfer brain patterns from one person to another. In this way, we can feel what others feel; we can empathize. What's more, when someone is communicating effectively they can get people's brains to actually synchronize. As you describe your yearnings, they become the yearnings of your listeners; when there is trouble, they gasp, and when longings are satisfied, your listeners smile. This is a powerful tool.

Stories take place in the imagination, and, to the human brain, imagined experiences are processed the same as real experiences. So we all go through the experience together, all on the same page. If this research is correct, then telling stories is a great way to build family bonds. Every family has tensions and grudges and disagreements. Chris and Sara always rub each other the wrong way, for example, and Jim and Randy have been arguing since the beginning of time. But tell a story to your family members, and for as long as you've got their attention, they are in your mind, and then they are WITH you. We all go through the experience together.

My father-in-law takes his role as family patriarch seriously. And let's face it, at 90, he has earned it. A bit stooped and slow moving, he is still sharp and overflowing with stories and advice. He painstakingly works his way to the front, and once there, he seems much bigger than his actual size.

Robert: *Okay, I want to tell you about many, many years ago when I was wooing this beautiful lady.* He gestures towards his wife Samantha, who beams.

After numerous overtures, she finally agreed to go out with me. She was living with her parents, Nicholas and Tessie Brown, in Queens and every time I called on her, I had to get by them.

Samantha corrects him on a particular detail and cheers him on from the sidelines with the same adoring eyes from 65 years ago. She loves the story but this does not stop her from adding corrections and additions to the story. *"Don't forget to tell them how I finally told you if you didn't propose soon, I was done with you!"*

Ian: *By the time we made it up the mountain, we were drenched in sweat. The fresh powder was nearly hip-deep all the way down the slope, just the way I like it. Finally at the top, we were ready to head down. This was the fun part! There was nothing but untracked mountain as far as we could see; no people, no trails, not even any footprints. Oh man, this was it, a perfect untouched run! But Zack was already exhausted, soaking wet, and terrified. He stood there staring down the mountain all the while shivering and crying that he could not do it. I was like, "What the f#*% is going on?"*

Jill: *If anyone has ever flown when 8-months pregnant, alone, with two little children, you know that I was near the end of my rope by the time we met the agent at our new rental. But as soon as I stepped across the threshold, I crossed into the world of despair. The place was old, ugly, moldy, in serious disrepair, and, on top of that, it was way too small for a family of five. But we had already paid the deposit, and we couldn't afford any more. I sat down and cried.*

We know the importance of empathy, the ability to understand and share the feelings of another. In this age of individualism, the ability to empathize becomes more necessary than ever. New research has uncovered the existence of "mirror neurons," which are neurons that react to emotions expressed by others and then reproduce these emotions. Oxytocin, the love hormone, is the neurochemical responsible for this phenomenon. It makes us more sensitive to social cues around us and motivates us to help others.

Mirror neurons provide us with an "embodied simulation" of not just the actions but the thoughts and feelings of other people. We actually share them physically. This is how stories connect us and transcend generations, grudges, and differences. Through stories, we share passions, sadness, hardships, and joys; we share meaning and purpose. They give us common ground that overcomes our defenses and our differences.

Our storytelling ability, a uniquely human trait, has been with us nearly as long as we've been able to speak. Across time and across cultures, stories have proved their worth not just as works of art or entertainment, but also as agents of personal and cultural transformation.

Robert: *So just around the time I was really starting to get serious about my honey, she presented me with a big surprise. It turned out she was a package deal. Samantha came with an adorable 3-year-old boy named Lee. It was all or nothing. My elegant date just turned into an exotic widow. Here I was, with no visible means of support, about to take the plunge into marriage and* *fatherhood all in one fell swoop! And she had already announced that there were other men interested and waiting. I couldn't risk losing her, so I jumped. And here I am.*

Ian: *"Come on Zack" I said "You can do this. Put on your skis and point them downhill." I tried to get him going but Zack shivered, and he was all like, "I can't, I can't". We were stuck on the top of this mountain, and the afternoon was closing in on us. So I did the only thing I could do—I slung him on my back, skis and all, and we all headed down.*

Kiara: *Somehow I found myself walking along the road. I have no idea how I got there. My former enthusiasm was gone, my legs were scratched and bleeding, and I was tired, so tired. I wondered what would happen to me. Yet through it all, I hoped if I kept going I would find my way back. The sun was still shining, but I thought I had been walking for hours. My mouth was so dry I could not swallow. My feet hurt. What if I never saw my parents again? I wanted to cry, but I was sure I was too old for that, so I kept walking.*

A car drove up and stopped beside me. A man leaned out the open window. "Hey little girl, are you lost?" He told me to get in. I knew I should not get in a stranger's car, and I did not like this man. I stood there unmoving. What if this was my only chance? He opened the door and the whoosh of cool air felt so good, and I was so tired. Just as I took a step closer to the car, a bike came barreling right up to me. "Daddy," I yelled. He threw down the bike and grabbed me up in his big arms and twirled me around in a bear hug.

We ended that evening with many requests for an encore show. There is no shortage of stories, and those moths are always searching for the lights to flap against, so I am guessing we will return with another act! We are, after all, each of us "once upon a time."

Kiara: *Just a quick PS: During my ordeal, my 3-year-old sister was heard to ask, "If she doesn't come back, can I have her Barbies?*

I will tell you something about stories—they aren't just entertainment. Don't be fooled. They are all we have, you see, all we have to fight off illness and death.
Leslie Marmon Silko

The Heart of Greenwich Village

The heart of Greenwich Village pulses with well-dressed college students in flowing scarves, tight jeans, soft leather boots, and designer t-shirts. It is like the Olsen twins times one thousand. Some are rushing by while others are draped casually outside the coffee shops and bookstores in animated conversations, cigarettes dangling, hands gesturing. My daughter Shanti is neither a professor nor a student. Believe it or not, she is in this urban site planting towering urns overflowing with beets and radishes.

A second population emerges: painters pushing shopping carts brimming with equipment, maintenance staff, and security guards. Mostly older men, many are recent immigrants, and all work here for New York University, which also employs Shanti. It does not take long before they are calling out to her, "Hey gardener lady, what you got to eat today? I brought my salad dressing."

One porter named George soon took ownership over the planters outside his building. Under his protection (don't sit on those plants, put your ciggies out somewhere else) and watering (not too wet, and not in the heat of midday), those pots overflowing with edibles and flowers have become the centerpieces of this cityscape.

Since she was a toddler, Shanti has been most content when her hands are in the earth and her head under an open sky. I remember when we were touring the Notre-Dame Basilica of Montreal, and she said, "I don't understand why people worship under this man made ceiling when the spirit of God comes so much closer in nature, on the hilltop, in the meadow, or on the ocean shore."

After starting Mantis, an organic farm, and operating a rapidly growing CSA in upstate NY back when she was twenty, Shanti went on to attend the prestigious School of Professional Horticulture at New York Botanical Gardens. Now she is a consultant for the University. "I see no need for the separation of ornamental and edible; beautiful flowers and delicious vegetables can and should co-exist. When I create green spaces, I am struck by the dramatic difference in the conversations," she explains. Passing newly planted flower beds, people make comments as they pass, 'beautiful', 'looking good', or 'how lovely', and they continue on their way. But when I am elbow deep in vegetable cultivation, the conversations tend to be longer and more engaged. 'What's going on?' 'Who's going to eat it?' 'That is the weirdest thing I have ever seen.' Then the personal stories begin: 'My grandfather grew beets. He came from the old country and always raised a few vegetables.' And we mustn't forget the offers, 'When are you going to harvest it? If nobody is going to eat it, I will.

We have become accustomed to passing boring expanses of lawn, but plant vegetables in the foreground and you can jolt people awake. Somehow the presence of the food we eat changes fleeting observations into personal conversation. Vegetables have long been hidden away in backyards and rural farms. We have no experience of vegetables in the public domain. Growing edible crops challenges the use of public space. Instead of a bench with a few flowers growing beside it, why not mesclun salad mix and edible flowers such as nasturtiums?

Eating food is one of our primary common needs, but is there a way to do this that is more visible and more connected to those of us who consume it? Planting vegetables can actually build community.

Food is a common denominator. We all eat, and most of us want fresh, healthy food for our families. Before people can take control of their health, they must begin to eat right. Creating health begins before that first bite is taken.

Local farmers' markets, too, are more than places to buy food. They're important parts of the community. Neighbors get to know one another, talk to the farmers, and learn about the food that is available. Studies have recently shown that people have ten times as many conversations at the farmer's market than they do at the supermarket.

"If I can grow food on West 49th Street, food can be grown anywhere in empty lots, on rooftops, in front porch planters, on suburban front lawns."

And she's right. From Michelle Obama in the White House to villagers in Zimbabwe, people want fresh, locally grown vegetables. According to the Burpee seed catalogue of 2006, 20% more people grew their own vegetables this year, bringing the number of gardeners in the US to 43 million.

I love watching Shanti at work. With one look at a space, she can see what it needs to be lush and vibrant and to put a soul at ease. It reminds me of Findhorn, an intentional commune of the '60s where Dorothy Maclean communicated with the cabbage spirits, and they grew gigantic plants in rather bleak conditions. I am not actually suggesting that Shanti is using magic, but there is a deep knowing, a comfort with growing green things that I see when I watch her in the plant world. Perhaps that is magic!

So bring your salad dressing and come on by! Shanti is the vibrant, dark-haired woman with work boots and dirty hands on the corner in Greenwich Village.

Addendum: Though she is no longer working for NYU, Shanti continues to make the world a more beautiful place. She is now the sole proprietor of Design Wild, a thriving business in New York City making gardens both public and private. Check out her website and her wonderful work www.designwildny.com.

Chairwoman of the Board

I was driving home with my teenage grandson when I answered a call from my post college nephew. Like so many 20-somethings these days, he has been busy figuring out his next step in the confusing, and often unsatisfying, job market. Should he stay in Colorado where he had a menial job but loved the hiking and the lifestyle? Should he take a high-powered job in New York City, a place he does not find hospitable? Or should he go to graduate school with a guarantee of more student loans but not of a resulting job. He talked, and I mostly listened, asking only a few questions. By the time the conversation was over, we had come up with a short list of next steps to keep him going in the right direction.

When I hung up, my grandson Jyasi turned to me and said, "You are like his personal advisor or guide. Wait a minute," he continued, "How many people do you do that for?"

Of course, I try to step in and help young people whenever I can. It's a confusing world. How are they to find the way forward? Maybe the words of Carlos Castaneda can help.

> Look at every path closely and deliberately.
> Try it as many times as you think necessary.
> Then ask yourself and yourself alone one
> question. Does this path have heart? If it does,
> the path is good. If it doesn't it is of no use.

But sometimes it is difficult to discern the heart along the way. That's when you need a little assistance. In fact, I believe that everyone needs at least one personal advisor, or better yet, their very own, custom-made board of directors. Organizations and corporations have a board to guide them, keep them moving in the right direction, balance their books, and bring their expertise to bear on all important decisions. Why shouldn't you and I have the same?

Well, it is possible. Start right now. Take out a pen and make a list of people you admire. They can be living or dead, personally known or famous, young or old, but they must be on that list for a reason. Either you admire them greatly, or they have a skill or ability that you know you could use. It could be a lawyer, an accountant, or an artist. She can be enthusiastic or clear thinking. I sometimes imagine what Maya Angelou or Tony Morrison would advise me or the joke that Nora Ephron would make at my expense to help me get over myself. But don't forget, you need some ready and willing flesh-and-blood people who will open the door when you knock late at night, put you in flannel jammies and give you a warm cup of hot cocoa and walk you through those dark places. Of course, keep in mind what Joseph Campbell said, "If the path before you is clear, you're probably on someone else's."

Red Lentil Soup Recipe

While you are assembling your own personal board of directors, I have a soup that will warm you right down to your toes and give you hope that the world will keep on ticking and the stars will keep on twinkling. The ingredients are usually in my pantry, and I can practically make it with my eyes closed while I am solving a myriad of more important problems. This soup comes out differently every time, but it can be on the table in less than 45 minutes where it will simmer with enticing aromas ready to guide you on your way.

Maybe we should call it Chairwoman of the Board soup!

All ingredients are approximate:

- A few tablespoons olive oil

- 1 large onion, chopped

- 2 or 3 garlic cloves, minced

- 2 tablespoons tomato paste or a can of tomatoes (we use our own jar)

- 2 teaspoons ground cumin

- 1/2 teaspoon salt

- Ground black pepper, to taste

- Cayenne, to taste

- Curry powder, optional

- Vegetable bouillon cube or vegetable broth

- 3 cups water

- 1 and 1/4 cup red lentils

- 1 large carrot, diced

- A green of your choice. Cabbage is really nice!

Preparation:
1. Heat the oil over high heat and sauté the onion and garlic until translucent.
2. Stir in tomatoes, cumin, salt, black pepper, chili powder, cayenne, or curry and sauté for a minute or two more.
3. Add broth, 2 cups water, lentils, carrot.
4. Simmer, then partially cover pot and turn heat to medium-low.
5. Simmer until lentils are soft, 20 or 30 minutes,
6. Add greens and simmer 10 minutes more.
7. Stir in lemon juice and cilantro.
8. Optional: Stir in juice of 1/2 lemon and chopped fresh cilantro

Praying with Our Feet

We cannot walk alone
And as we walk
We must make the pledge
That we shall always march ahead
We cannot turn back.
                    Martin Luther King Jr. III

My small group of friends and family left Harlem around 10:30 AM and walked fifty blocks through the top of beautiful Central Park down to 72nd street. As we walked and watched people pass us by, we wondered—*Are they going where we are going? Will anybody be there?* There were very few folks around, which made us doubtful, but when we finally climbed out of the park at 72nd street; we were embraced by a hot, sweaty sea of surging humanity. So many had come!

The clarion call had gone out. With Martin Luther King's words to inspire us, we gathered to put our bodies on the street and march, to say, "Pay attention! The time is growing late! We must protect this planet!"
From far and wide we came.
By bike and boat, train and bus.
On bike and skateboard and foot, we came.
Young and old, rich and poor,
English speakers or not, we came.
Brown and white, black, red and yellow, we came.
Gay and bi, trans and straight, we came.
Carrying signs, carrying babies, carrying art, banging drums, calling chants, we came.

The sun was shining, the streets ahead were cleared of cars, the police were out in quantity, and the elaborate, yearlong organizational work of 350.org and many others was impeccable. We wore bright t-shirts declaring our organizations, our schools, our churches, and our justice groups. We wore shimmering capes, saris, and superhero costumes. A young woman in our group sported a colorful cape covered in the names and handprints of her preschool students, so she could bring them all to the march with her. We carried banners and signs and globes declaring:

KEEP THE OIL IN THE GROUND!
PROTECT MOTHER EARTH!
DENIAL IS NOT A CLIMATE POLICY!
DIVEST IN FOSSIL FUELS!
IT'S GETTING HOT IN HERE! TAKE OFF ALL YOUR COALS!

> We chanted:
> *Tell me what you want!*
> *Justice!*
> *Tell me when you want it!*
> Now!
>
> *Hey Hey, Ho,Ho! Fossil fuels have got to go!*
> *Hey Hey. Ho Ho!*

There were those who meditated for climate justice. South of Columbus Circle, about two dozen people sat on the park hillside overlooking the street. They were cloaked in a deep, peaceful silence as they sat cross-legged and still.

For the first hour, as we waited to actually start marching, I was thrilled, but then I became overwhelmed. The crowds, the heat, the activity. I was already hot and tired from our long walk down, and I considered packing it in and going back. But my daughter, always the one with brilliant uncommon sense, moved me a block away from the crowd where we found a little space and a breeze. It calmed me down.

We miraculously met up with friends from Boston, my nephew and a group of young people connected to Shanti and Avi in the city. Then we waited. And we waited, and waited.

After more than an hour, the cheers went up, and we began to move forward. Chanting, singing, and walking, we marched. It was truly a walking prayer. I understood the words Rabbi Abraham Joshua Heschel spoke when he marched in 1960 with Martin Luther King in Selma. "Legs are not lips and walking is not kneeling. And yet our legs uttered songs. Even without words, our march was worship. I felt my legs were praying."

At 12:58, there was a moment of silence to honor those already suffering from the effects of climate change. Silence rolled toward us like a tidal wave. It had dimension and weight. Tears came too. Imagine being in the midst of hundreds of thousands of people in almost complete and utter silence. It was mind-blowing and a truly holy experience. After a minute, a thunder of sound covered us as the entire forty blocks erupted in cheers and calls, and yells and whistles.

Late that afternoon, with about ten blocks still to go to the finishing area, we thought about peeling off. It did not bother me to leave a little before the end, but I really wanted a glimpse of Bill McKibben. Literally two blocks after I said that, Bill appeared. There on the sidewalk in his bright red 350.org t-shirt with only a few people around him. There stood the tall, skinny pilot light of the climate movement. I went over and thanked him!

There are so many days when I am overwhelmed with despair for our planet. I worry it is too late and that the corporate forces are too big, too greedy, and too powerful. We have dragged our feet for far too long, the earth is already dying, thousands of plants and animals have been driven to extinction, and the oceans, the air, and the earth are all polluted. The list goes on and on. But on this day, there was only hope and triumph in the air. As we turned onto 6th Avenue and headed down 42nd street, giant screens flashed video of throngs of people in Australia, India, Tibet, and Brazil marching with us. One hundred and sixty-two countries all over the world held similar rallies. Two million, six hundred thousand people were marching! Marching, marching, marching. Martin Luther King, Jr. said, "We must build dikes of courage to hold back the flood of fear". Our feet marched and the dikes rose up to hold back the flood of rising waters of fear and despair. Marching, marching, marching. I imagined Arundhati Roy whispering in my ear, "Another world is not only possible, she is on her way. On a quiet day I can hear her breathing."

By four in the afternoon, we were asked to go home. The final gathering place was over capacity. And here, at the weary end of my day of social activism, is where I was almost arrested. The barricades lining the streets were everywhere, making it almost impossible to leave the march. But it was time to go, so I climbed

259

over. Suddenly five policemen converged on me. My kids had given me the boost, but they quickly backed away and marched on leaving me alone and surrounded. Yikes. I was just trying to go home. I picked out the one lady cop and said, "I am an old lady, and I need to pee." She smiled (only a little) and walked on. A little white lie, but I do usually need to pee.

Next stop: We gathered at a Ramen shop for the biggest, most delicious bowl of hot, vegetable ramen. That should be a required food for all marchers. My feet hurt, my shoulders ached, but I felt so GOOD!

> *First they ignore you*
> *Then they laugh at you*
> *Then they fight you*
> *Then you win*
> Mahatma Gandhi

Motorboat, Motorboat Move So Slow

Wisdom is a funny thing. To gain it is like catching a fish with your bare hands—it is alive and slithery, and just when you think you have it in your grasp, it flips, flops, and is gone. But for that split second when you feel it grasped, hopefully between your sweaty palms, there is a moment of exhilaration, an I've-got-this moment! And then it squirms away, and you are left empty-handed and foolish wondering what just happened. (Okay, the truth is I have never caught a fish in my bare hands unless you count my goldfish, and that was with a yogurt container. Needless to say, the fish was not happy about it.)

Renting a boat on a little pastoral canal in the French countryside was a little like trying to catch wisdom. Lee gets these ideas, and then, like a pit bull with a bone, he will not let go. So even though we knew nothing about boats or navigation, off we went to Mijennes. There, after promising our first born as a security deposit, a wiry man gave us a ten-minute boat lesson in a foreign language and had us sign a waiver of all rights and a damage note. He then leapt off the deck, abandoning us on the water in a strange vehicle that had no wheels or brakes just as we were approaching a lock. Maybe you are comfortable with fore and aft and all that Tally Ho nonsense, but I am a land creature. I love water—river, stream, lake, or sea— as long as I am gazing upon it from shore. Unless it is a bathtub! Then I am happy to climb aboard. Otherwise, I am content to leave Ahab to his adventures with not even a shred of envy. You won't ever catch me on a

261

cruise ship and those are practically beaches in slow motion.

And yet, somehow, I ended up as the sole crewmember on what was, without a doubt, a boat (it had ropes, an anchor, and it was in the water) even though it was clumsy, slow moving, and more like a floating dock with bumpers.

We soon mastered moving forward with impressive agility and eventually figured out how to go backwards, which was considerably more challenging. It was too cold for any other boaters to venture out, so except for a couple of swans, we had no river traffic to contend with. This turned out to be exceptionally propitious since our boating dexterity was awkward at best. There was however—add ominous soundtrack here—the locks. If this had been where the Loch Ness monster came from, it would have all made sense.

These locks are not a natural phenomenon. Years ago, someone in France with a Napoleonic complex had this crazy idea to fling locks about like breadcrumbs to swans on this otherwise idyllic river. Purring along, feeling proud and competent in our floating putt-putt until, there in the distance, the next lock appeared waiting malevolently to humble us and turn my knees to jelly and my belly to a queasy bubbling cauldron. Each lock was different, and so each approach must be calculated. We had to figure how and where to tie up and if the water was going up or down (sometimes 16 feet). Maneuvering past the arrogant lock attendants, who only spoke FRENCH (how dare they!) left us comically fraught and anxious.

There I was with my creaky knees and sensitive back leaping off the boat with the rope in hand to tie up and pull us in as the lock changed. But you can't actually tie up when the boat drops those 16 or so feet because you would be left hanging, a thought that filled me with fresh terror each day. Instead, you have to loop (is that the nautical term?) the line. I proudly hooked the front (is it bow?), and just as I was congratulating my nimble self, the back (starboard?) would swing wildly out to sea. This was definitely not the peaceful vacation cruise I pictured complete with white-gloved porters and multi-coursed elegant meals.

Did I mention that I was shanghaied? For you earth-plodders, shanghaied is a nautical term from way back, and it means to be involuntarily pressed into service on a ship. I was! It may have gotten me a few days in Paris, but that first day on the water jumping fore to aft, lassoing docks, squinting ahead for lock openings, navigating by water maps, and don't forget working in the galley, had me exhausted. Have you ever prepared three meals a day in a 2×2 space with rationed amounts of water and a scarcity of cutlery, all the while rocking back and forth? Forget Julia Child and gourmet French cuisine. Simple bread and cheese would have to do.

But when I stopped shivering (each morning we chopped ice off the boat), I admired the pastoral fields of yellow rapeseed, the tall cypress, and lilacs dipping blooming boughs into their river reflections. The locks, though never mastered, got a little easier. You should have seen me by the end, leaping fore and aft like a graceful gazelle as Lee perched proudly behind the wheel!

The pirates of the Caribbean have nothing on me. After reenacting Pirates of the Bourgogne canals, I am ready for the next adventure. I just hope it is on land. Camels across Mongolia anyone?

They Walk Among Us

I collect Bodhisattvas. They walk unnoticed among us. I know they do. I am always on the lookout. They could be anywhere, and it is difficult to discern who they are. She could be the weary cashier behind that spinning bag holder at Walmart or the slouched guy with pimples who wheels in the giant garbage can to sweep up your spilled popcorn at the movie theater. Who knows? He could even be your banker in his three-piece suit or maybe that perky, blonde Pilates instructor. I know that they live near us, but they're quite shy. Don't look at them straight on. You kind of have to sneak a peek out of the corner of your eye. They try to blend in.

A Bodhisattva is an ordinary person who moves in the direction of the Buddha. It is someone who has compassion for all sentient beings. Most of us regular people live thinking and reacting to our own personal, narrow circumstances while a Bodhisattva, though still ordinary, lives as if the fate of all humanity rests within her and is her responsibility. You see, they have chosen to stay on earth for another go 'round rather than achieve enlightenment right now. They do this for the sake of you and me, patiently waiting for us to catch up.

What is all this hoo-ha about enlightenment anyway? Matthieu Ricard, a French physicist, writer and Buddhist monk, says that enlightenment is a state of perfect knowledge or wisdom combined with infinite compassion. The Buddha himself once explained concisely what is meant by an enlightened one or Buddha:

What has to be known, that I have known;
What has to be abandoned, that I have abandoned;
What has to be developed, that I have developed;
Therefore, O Brahmin, I am a Buddha.

You can see, that he is kind of done on this earthly plain. Jiko, the great grandmother Buddhist nun in *For the Time Being*, by Ruth Ozeki is a bodhisattva. She explains the meaning of it in simple terms: she will not get on the elevator until everyone else is on. Imagine that. It is common courtesy. We have to all get ready and achieve enlightenment together. It is much the same way that the earth must be healed for us all—animals and people, democrats and republicans, evangelical and atheist.

But maybe enlightenment is simply living your life to the best of your ability, acting from your highest self as much as possible. Maybe it is about striving and not necessarily achieving.

Some of the Bodhisattvas have become well known. They practically throb with gentle power. Think of Bishop Tutu who led the Peace and Reconciliation Commission in South Africa. Have you ever heard his delighted laugh? After all he's witnessed and been through during apartheid, that laugh is a sure sign. What about Wangari Maathai, founder of the Green Belt Movement, planting hundreds of trees in Kenya and undergoing beatings and arrests to do it. I think she might be one.

Or there is Ina May Gaskin who has done for natural, healthy childbirth what Steve Jobs did for something else (what was it?). Of course, we have Amy Goodman, a tireless voice of independent journalism, who presents an unvarnished truth every day. And Sima Simar, a woman doctor in Afghanistan who continually risks her life for the human rights of girls and women. They might very well be Bodhisattva. Those are a few who have managed to garner some awards, but most live unobtrusively, just doing the right thing, what is needed. It is as normal to them as breathing. Like my friend Ardi who took in her suddenly orphaned niece to raise as a member of the family. Or soft-spoken Evie teaching nursery school for thirty years with strength and bounteous love. She gave many children a dynamic start to their learning adventure and then she did it for their brothers and sisters and for their children.

Another one who comes to mind is Jeff, a teacher in an underfunded Detroit school where the walls are crumbling, the books are dog-eared, and the kids are worn down. He energetically strives to awaken the young men and women to a world of inquiry and mostly tries to keep them out of the bullets' range.

Can you look around and add a few possibilities to my list? If you pay attention, I think you will find them in the most unexpected places.

It turns out, wouldn't you know it, that there are Bodhisattvas described in the ancient Hebrew teachings. They are called the Lamed Vav Tzadikim or righteous souls. It is said that at all times there must be thirty-six of these special people in the world. Were it not for them, and it must be all of them, if even one of them is missing, the world would come to an end. The Lamed-Vavniks do not themselves know that they are one of the thirty-six. In fact, it is said that should a person claim to be one that is proof positive that they are certainly not. Since the thirty-six are each exemplars of *anavah* (humility), that precludes them from proclaiming their place among the special righteous. The thirty-six are simply too humble to believe that they are one of the thirty-six.

But the real kicker is this: because we do not know who they are, we must treat everyone as if they might be a holy person! And because, amazing though it might be, we might, ourselves, be one, we must even treat ourselves as we would treat a saint. Think about that for a moment. How would that affect the world? How would it change my actions? If the Dalai Lama or the Pope might be the man changing my oil or topping off my mocha latte, or the Virgin Mary was checking out my groceries, maybe I would act differently. I might choose to meet the world from my highest self; I might finally pay attention.

With this in mind, I made a decision. I am starting a sky club for Bodhisattvas or Lamed-Vavniks. They do walk among us, and maybe they need occasional awards, recognition, or frequent flyer miles. We can keep it on the down low. Just a simple nod or a thumbs up as we pass them by. Maybe a plate of homemade cookies now and then so they know they are not forgotten. I am looking for nominations. Keep your eyes open and send them in.

> *humanity i love you*
> *because you are perpetually*
> *putting the secret of life*
> *into your pants and forgetting it's there*
> *and sitting down on it*
> e e cummings

Wall of Hope

Quite a few years ago, I had an adorable young niece. Her name is Zena and I still have her but she is not quite so young or adorable anymore. Well, okay, she is still adorable. But back then, Wednesday was our special day. Her parents both worked full time, so she and I had Wednesday afternoons together. I picked her up from day care or later from school. We found plenty of things to do. We shopped, cleaned, cooked, gardened and did projects: baking, crafts, painting. Zena has a steadiness and competence that makes everything right and fun. Somewhere along the way we created a special project that took on a life of its own.

It started at the local hardware store. I headed to the sawmill where I asked them to cut a ¼ inch 4x8 piece of plywood into 4x4 squares. The squares came home in a box, and we were ready to start. Using craft paints, we each painted a square. We began with turtles and kitties. Then we moved onto scenes of mountains and houses and oceans and flowers. Next we focused on faces—beautiful people gazing back at us. Finally we tried Matisse-like abstracts. We were obsessed with our vibrant tiles, and we invited anyone under 20-years old who stepped through our front door to join in. My young grandchildren asked to paint one every time they came over. Friends of Avi, my teenage son, joined in, and a few over-20s begged for a chance. That Thanksgiving, I packed up the paints and some blank tiles and flew to Colorado where my nieces and nephews out there quickly got involved.

Eventually, after painting all the raw edges and applying a coat of polyurethane, it was time to hang the tiles. We found the perfect place: our stairway wall leading to the second floor. Zena and I arranged them and rearranged them on the floor. There were considerations: color contrast, artist, and subject matter. What pleasure we got from that joyous kaleidoscope of colors gazing back at us.

With the help of tile paste and a few spacers, the tiles soon covered our stairwell in dazzling eye-catching splendor. They reach almost to the ceiling, and seem to call out a greeting to all who enter.

A friend saw the display and asked if I would teach an in-service at the children's mental health unit where she worked. I agreed, as long as Zena could co-teach it with me. After all, she co-created the project, and no one knew better how to make it work. We taught that in-service with lots of examples and technical solutions. They subsequently created a "Wall of Hope" where each child on the unit made a tile before being discharged.

I think it may be true that everyone needs a wall of hope! You do not have to cover a stairwell or plaster it across your entry. It could be on your refrigerator, in a corner of your bedroom, or on a bathroom wall. It doesn't even have to be a wall. What gives you hope and allows you to take a deep breath and smile? Think of something, someone, or words that help you to remember that you belong here in this world and that there is kindness and forgiveness and beauty waiting just on the other side of your next breath. Something that reminds you of the fierce beauty and terrible kindness of this one world we share. And then place that reminder where you can't miss it on those days when despair is knocking on your front door.

Zena recently graduated college and jumped into law school. She has lots of brilliant plans that only rarely include me. But she will always be part of my wall of hope. I only have to remind myself or hear her voice. Now I babysit for my new grandson, Niko, on Wednesday afternoons. There must be some Karmic magic to Wednesdays for me. I wonder what project we will take on. Right now, we are limited to chewable projects —blocks, books, and biscuits all seem to work. But speaking of hope, he just started to walk, so anything is possible!

Beam Me Up Scottie

I love to fly. I get excited just boarding a plane knowing that I'll soon arrive in some new place. My wanderlust has diminished a little as I grow older, and I find that sitting still in a few square feet of space, strapped in and breathing that reprocessed air feels less and less comfortable. But boarding that winged tin can still equates with adventure and freedom. My heart opens wide and my mind stands to attention. I am fully alive. Anything is possible: people to meet, food to try, and adventure awaits. I think traveling is a superfood; it amps up mindfulness, builds fellowship, and develops the life-force.

I have a longstanding prayer practice for take-off and landing. It is not exactly fear or faith that has me praying on every voyage, but a form of wonder. Somewhere along the way, I came to believe that I should help the pilot fly the plane at take-off and at landing. After all, why should we take it for granted that that 500-ton tub of metal, upholstery, bags of pretzels, and human beings should be able to rise into the sky? And then a few hours later, at the scheduled time, in the right place, we expect it to land its huge ungainly mass smoothly down upon the waiting tarmac. It really is a truly awesome event. We should be surprised and astonished every time it happens as if a miracle had occurred. That is why, many years and dozens of flights ago, I began to recite the Shema at takeoff and landing. It doesn't take long—just the time from taxing down the runway until being aloft and level in the sky. And it is not intrusive even in that cramped space, though I do actually sing it out loud. I allow the engine noise to mask most of my warbling.

The great Mahatma Gandhi always chanted "Ramanama", which can be translated as "Oh God," as he went about his day. He said, "This incantation of Rama will free you from addictions, make you clean, and everyone will adore you. Your whole day will pass happily, and your nights will be free from bad dreams if you take Rama after you get up in the morning and before you go to sleep at night."

It sounds like a mighty effective nutritional supplement. It was an ongoing meditation, a practice of mindfulness. He quietly chanted those words as he walked with kings into the halls of parliament. He spoke them under his breath as he sat in a dusty village before a spinning wheel. He chanted in jail as he lay prostrate with dehydration brought on by long hunger fasts. They were said to be his last words when a man leaped out of the crowd and shot him. The shots rang out and muffled the sound of Gandhi's softly chanted words. It has been said that those are the only words necessary to take you right up to God, as if Gandhi needed any help with that!

In the same way, in the Jewish tradition the Shema is supposed to be the words you recite at death. It is not exactly that I believe I am going to die in that plane, but the truth is, I am a little closer to heaven when I am up there, and it never hurts to hedge your bets.

Years ago, thinking of all this, I began to prepare myself. I tried chanting Rama, Rama, Rama, Gandhi's Hindu chant. I tried Om Mani Padme Hum, the ancient Tibetan Buddhist mantra that when spoken out loud invokes the blessings of Chenrezig, the embodiment of compassion. I tried The Lord is My Shepherd, a truly beautiful verse but one with a lot of "he's" in it. I even tried Ek Ong Kar, a gift from Guru Nanak to the Sikhs. I tried them all, but nothing seemed to stick. Until one day, the Schema found me. Maybe it was my namesake, Great Grandma Eva poking me from the beyond and reminding me, "Don't forget, you are Jewish. It is deep in your bones. It was there when your grandmother left the old world to come to a strange land. It was there when we sang 'Sunrise Sunset' as we buried your father. You have a kinship to these ancient Hebrew prayers." And, so, the Schema and I have reunited.

The Schema is "Shema Yisrael" or "Hear, O Israel", the first two words of a section of the Torah, and the prayer that serves as a centerpiece of the morning and evening Jewish prayer services. The root "sh-m-a" means to hear, to pay attention, to understand, and to respond. Not much to argue with there. Mindfulness is all about attention. Observant Jews consider the Shema to be the most important part of the prayer service, and its twice-daily recitation is a *mitzvah* (religious commandment). It is traditional for parents to teach their children to say it before they go to sleep at night. And Jews, like Gandhi with Rama, hope to say the Shema as their last words upon dying.

The first verse is:

שְׁמַע יִשְׂרָאֵל יְיָ אֱלֹהֵינוּ יְיָ אֶחָד

Sh'ma Yis'ra'eil Adonai Eloheinu Adonai echad.
Hear, Oh Israel, the Lord is our God,
the Lord is One.

I can't read the Hebrew, but I like how it looks. And how profound is that? The Lord is one. That means

273

male or female, bi or trans, black, white, brown, yellow, or red. It means Jew, Christian, or Muslim. It means you and me. All is one. Sometimes I even get to the second verse. *Barukh sheim k'vod malkhuto l'olam va'ed.* Blessed be the Name of His glorious kingdom for ever and ever. I cannot think of a better time to bless her Queendom than right now when we are polluting and heating it to within an inch of its life.

I am not a very educated or active Jew, but I figure that the Shema is there for any of us, and so I do kind of help myself to it. I don't wish to offend anyone, but I figure it is lodged somewhere deep in my bloodstream. I know it goes at least as far back to the Russian shtetl where my ancestors recited it, and I guess it was there when Moses crossed the Red Sea. So far, it has worked wonders for me. Every single plane I have been on where I have sung the Shema, has taken off and landed safely. Not bad! That's an impressive record of success!

I often have to stop lively conversations with newly introduced seat mates and take a singing time-out while I help to get this plane aloft. Sometimes, I offer a short explanation to my neighbor; mostly I just turn toward the window and sing softly. The droning engines almost covers my trembling notes. But sing I do, right up into the skies!

So if you are sitting next to a somewhat nondescript older woman at your next flight, and you catch a little muffled crooning at take-off and hear fragments of words you might not understand, that is just me singing our airplane into the sky.

Ballast not Bucket

You would have to have been on another planet to not know about the viral tidal wave called the Ice Bucket challenge, a charitable show of support for ALS victims that had multitudes of people dousing themselves with a bucket full of ice water. It made millions for ALS and may have forever changed the way charity fundraising is approached. Kim Kardashian did it, Bill Gates did it, George W. Bush did it, and even the Simpsons did it. They poured a bucket full of ice water and ice cubes on their heads, all for a good cause. I still wonder why this captured the attention of so many people here in the United States.

But watching all that water being dumped out, I began to worry. We are, you know, experiencing serious drought in many places throughout our planet? Was there no awareness that many people in the world do not have access to safe drinking water? What must it be like for them to see gallons of clean water getting thrown away over famous heads? "It's basically narcissism masked as altruism," said Pardes from Vice Magazine. I tend to agree. But this ice bucket hoo-ha brought me back to something else I had been thinking about not too long before. No, not the polar bear swim and not an ice-cold margarita. But rather to bucket lists.

I think these bucket lists have a similar theme of excess. Do you remember when bucket lists became all the rage? Everyone was making them, each item wilder than the previous one.

1. Climb Mt Everest.
2. Sail around the world.

3. Become President of Mongolia.

Bucket lists tend to be wild and wonderful and full of me, me, me. People were actually manifesting them, checking the items off their list one by one and then making new ones. Some even tried to outdo others with bigger, more sensational and more daring lists. There are entire websites dedicated to this.

In fact, they even made a movie called *The Bucket List*. It featured two old codgers played by Jack Nicholson and Morgan Freeman. Those guys can make even a dumb movie appealing. One rich and spoiled (guess who? Hint: think white) and one hardworking and sincere. They meet in chemotherapy treatment and discuss their unfulfilled dreams. And then (not a big surprise) they go off to make those fantasies happen one by one. In the end (spoiler alert), Freeman returns to his wife choosing to be content with what he has, and Nicholson just goes on and on.

Maybe it is the wisdom of the years, or maybe it is the fact that we boomers have gobbled up so many resources and are leaving the legacy of a polluted, overheated planet that is deep in crisis to our grandchildren, but recently I had this idea that it was time to popularize letting go. Rather than grabbing more, we could start to aim for cleaning out our lives. We could all make a list of the things we no longer need to aim for, grab, and consume.

Author Marie Kondo's books *Spark Joy* and *The Life Changing Magic of Tidying Up* tackle part of the issue I am discussing and have become best sellers. Ms. Kondo runs a consulting business in Tokyo to help clients transform their cluttered homes into spaces of serenity and inspiration. The basic concept is to surround yourself only with things that spark joy. Decide what you want to keep, not necessarily what you want to throw away.

Once you clean out your belongings, you will naturally want to clean out your bucket list too! How? It turns out is as easy as 1-2-3—a simple check mark, and it is GONE. Talk about simplicity and decluttering. There might be a lightness and pleasure in this. My bucket list was weighing me down; it was an anchor around my neck. Maybe I was sinking under the weight.

Then I decided to make a *Ballast List*. My daughter suggested that it was really a "fuck-it" list, but for now I will stick with ballast. Ballast is a nautical term describing the heavy gravel used to provide stability in sea-going boats. If a boat does not have enough ballast, it will tip in high winds and might even capsize. The biggest ships use seawater as additional ballast, and as they get close to harbor, they drain the seawater ballast from their holds and come in to port much lighter, floating higher on the water, and making it much easier to maneuver. Sigh. I want to glide higher in the water of life as I float into a safe harbor.

A few years after I began thinking about my ballast list, I saw an article in the Sunday Times with "Bucket List" as its title. I thought that someone had the same idea as I had, and maybe it would soon be a cultural phenomenon. Upon reading, I discovered the article was about horrible experiences that people wished never again to experience, such as being hit by a car, bitten by a rat, or trapped on a broken subway. Well, duh, I could see why they did not want to repeat those disasters. They called it a bucket list in reverse. But this is not the same thing as a Ballast List.

277

So instead of filling and hoarding buckets, how about getting rid of those extra, sinking burdens and tossing some ballast overboard? What if we chose not to stockpile stuff, desires, and even adventures? Instead of more, we could go deeper, slower, and finer. We might have more space and time to savor and discern. We could watch the sunrise and take ambling strolls.

It's a good thing my husband has not read this. He has BIG plans. Adventure is his middle name. Don't worry; we do not have to forego all adventure. Just, well you know, f#*k it!

OKAY, I'll go first.

1. I am not going to trek in Nepal. I used to imagine circumnavigating Annapurna and gazing up at the stars in the cold night sky, but no, I toss Annapurna out of the bucket. Sigh.
2. I am not going to ride that new faster roller coaster.
3. I am not going to skydive.
4. I am not going to run a marathon.
5. I am not going to have a mother who adores me.
6. I am not going to speak fluent Spanish.

Hey, I am beginning to feel lighter already. I think this will allow me to be more present. But don't think I am going to curl up and play bingo all day. I might, however, watch the birds, take some deep breaths, and be a better friend. I don't plan to empty my bucket. Oh no. I still have dreams. But some well-planned decluttering is an excellent idea. I will soon be floating so much higher in the water.

Happy Birthday to You

Children's birthdays are wonderful, aren't they? Well, they are usually portrayed that way with overflowing adoration, mounds of cake and ice cream, and of course, piles of presents. But has anyone else noticed that the birthday party tradition might be getting out of control? Rather than the life-affirming event we imagine it to be, it now reminds me of *The Clay Pot Boy*, a fairy tale where a childless elderly couple bakes a little pot boy. Coming to life, he marches through the village devouring everything in his path. But he can't get enough food to satisfy his ever expanding hunger. Even as he eats and grows larger, he bellows, "I'm hungry, I'm hungry!"

The typical children's birthday party involves a dozen sweet cherubs, scrubbed and smiling, who soon morph into screaming monsters while the honored birthday host tears into a towering pile of gifts like a blood-crazed piranha. What are we teaching our children? Studies show that children who are given too much grow into adults who have difficulty coping. They become more vulnerable to depression and anxiety and have difficulty in work and relationships.

I admit that I tried to wrestle with these issues when my children were young, and I too failed to tame the party monster. But this year, I attended my grandson's birthday party and while a more wonderful child you may never meet, the carnage of acquisition was more than I could bear. There were altogether too many presents for one little 5-year old to process at a time.

I'm not the only person recoiling from the feeding frenzy. I have been conducting a survey of parents, grandparents, aunts, and uncles asking, "What do you think of children's birthday party experience?" Well the results are in, and guess what? Many people have become wary of the custom. Yet it seems that everyone feels helpless to stop it.

So I want to start a movement: Bridle the Birthday Bash. My 10-year-old niece, Zena, thinks it's a good idea. She suggests we call it *Grandma's Treasures* or *2U x 2*. Basically, there would be a website that lists children's organizations and orphanages all over the world that need toys, clothes, games, and dollars. Parents and children could sign on and be matched to a worthy cause somewhere. Together they would send items and checks, write illustrated notes, enclose photographs, and build a personal connection with the organization they are helping. Someday they might even go visit. At the party, everyone would participate in giving to that child's chosen organization in the birthday boy or girl's name. In this way, we could expand the meaning in our children's lives while the parties themselves would become more social and meaningful.

What do you think? Can we rein in this monster and put the magic back in birthdays? Remember the *Clay Pot Boy* in the story? As he rampages through the village eating everything, he grows larger and larger, but he is still hungry. Eventually he turns and eats the old couple. He calls out, "I'm hungry, I'm hungry." After he eats the old man and the old woman, the farmer, the woodsman, the bull, and others, he is ready to eat a little goat with curly horns. She says, "Wait until I get up on a hill so I can run right into your mouth." At the top of the hill, the plucky goat lowers her horns, charges down the hill and crashes into the clay pot boy. He shatters leaving everything he devoured standing whole amid the shards.

Now I'm not claiming to have grown a pair of horns, but I think there are a lot of plucky parents and grandparents out there who could smash this birthdays-run-amuck creature into smithereens. How about it? Care to join me? What a birthday gift it would be!

Honking Geese

The x-ray was right there in the light box in front of me but my eyes were on the face of the pulmonary specialist, a hotshot doctor who happened to be a friend of my brother. After herding me over to see the x-ray, he was bombarding me with complex explanations. The words sailed past my head like a flock of honking geese. I already knew; I knew with a leaden certainty. There would be no good news arriving this day. My younger brother Peter was dying. ... and he was dying fast.

The hospital room down the hall became Peter's new headquarters. He had arrived there following three weeks of various rounds of antibiotics prescribed to treat a resistant pneumonia which we finally knew he did not have. During the month of August he went from being a powerful tennis player who biked long distances and worked full time to being a hospital patient barely able to climb a few stairs. By the time I was looking at the x-ray, he was struggling for each breath.

That was the day; the big C-Day. They told us that he had Stage 4 Adenocarcinoma non-small cell lung cancer. Here he was, one of the few people in the world who had never smoked a cigarette, never had a beer or even a cup of coffee. And no, he was not a purist, he just never liked them. He claimed that those facts were always good when he played "Two Truths and a Lie". No one ever guessed that those statements could actually be the truth. There was no rhyme or reason to this diagnosis. Tragedy is not always a rational partner. It can sneak up and leave you flattened like the oblivious road runner tooling down the road sure he will run on forever. My brother, truly the best of my family, was supposed to be around for a long time.

We heard the diagnosis, the death knell, but we couldn't take it in. He would be the exception, we thought, he would beat this. Of course I knew it was a bad prognosis, but miracles happen every day. Why shouldn't we expect one? We would think positively. Peter turned to Kiara and quietly said, "I may never work again." And a chill of real foreboding ran through me. He mentioned the new program he was about to launch with the Albany Police department and the mediation class for law students that began later in the month. Who would do them?

Given the diminished returns on chemo at this stage, Peter chose to forego the traditional treatment. At its best it might gain him a couple of months, but at the cost of hospital stays, nausea and worse. If you go with the medically prescribed protocol, it is fairly straightforward; there are few decisions to make. Go or stop is basically the entire scope. But in the world of alternative treatments the options are almost unlimited. The task of sorting through the possibilities under urgent time pressure was nearly overwhelming. This is where the family committee came in. More on that in a moment, but first some good news!

After six grim weeks filled with frantic research into possible treatment protocols, and new normals consisting of rapidly increasing accommodations for Peter, such as oxygen tanks and commodes, we finally had something to celebrate. Unfortunately it didn't have anything to do with Peter. Moses's partner, Joanna, gave birth to a healthy baby boy. This perfect new being entered the world just in time to remind us of life's miraculous ebb and flow. The swaddled infant could soon be found in Peter's arms, curled up around the oxygen tubes.

Not until naming him Niko did Moses realize that his own middle name, Nicholas, was after his paternal grandfather. That discovery was only the first. In the weeks following his arrival, little Niko led us on a fascinating ancestral treasure hunt. His name comes from Tsar Nicholas of Russia, who is, of course, White Russian royalty. Moses felt the need to balance that elitism by bestowing a middle name from red Russian or working class roots. The search for a middle name soon brought him to my side of the family.

Dipping into the history of Russian activists, Moses unearthed the renowned Doctor, Antoinette Konikow. Now, Konikow is not a common name, but it was my mother's maiden name. Indeed it turns out that Antoinette was the first wife of my grandfather, Moses Konikow, my son's other namesake. We knew he was a doctor and an activist in Boston, but he died when my mother was only 10 so none of us had ever met him or even heard many stories about him. We knew only the bare outline: he came to Boston from eastern Russia: he had a previous marriage and two older children; he fought for women's rights and birth control with the famous Margaret Sanger, the founder of Planned Parenthood.

We soon made contact with Antoinette's granddaughter in California and discovered that Moses Konikow and his first wife, Antoinette, were both physicians trained in Switzerland. They were also followers of Trotsky who believed passionately in workers' rights. They both worked tirelessly to bring birth control to women. In those days, the early 1900's, it was illegal for a doctor to so much as offer a patient advice on ways to avoid a pregnancy, even if she already had 13 children and nothing to feed them. My eight-year old mother sometimes helped her father make diaphragms by pouring rubber into molds in the basement, though she did not know exactly what they were for. The two doctors developed a spermicidal jelly to go with the diaphragms and they secretly distributed both throughout the US, Europe and even Russia. Antoinette wrote a famous book, *Voluntary Motherhood*, a concept that, in itself, was a radical and dangerous proposal.

Like many Jewish immigrants around the turn of the century, they were part of the Workmen's Circle. The Workmen's Circle was founded in 1892 on New York's Lower East Side by a handful of Jewish sweatshop workers as a mutual aid society. Despite its name, two of the first members were women! This small society grew to over 80,000 members by 1920. Helping its members to adapt to their new life in America, it provided life insurance, unemployment relief, healthcare, social interaction, burial assistance and a general education about life in their new country. Members cultivated a diverse and inclusive community that was rooted in Jewish culture and social action rather than in orthodox religion. This was a radical departure from the previous generation in the old country.

Because of the Russian pogroms in the 1880s and succeeding decades, more than 2 million Yiddish-speaking Jews fled Eastern Europe with their families, and most immigrated to the United States, arriving destitute at Ellis Island in New York City. Many of them entered the fast-growing, but exploitative garment industry. This was true of all of our grandparents on both my side and Lee's, except for my grandfather Moses who entered this country as a physician.

By gleaning information from Antoinette's granddaughter and a few of my cousins we learned all this and also that both doctors volunteered every summer at the Workmen's Circle summer camp as the camp doctors.

So in the long family tradition of community organizing, practically the first thing we did after hearing Peter's diagnosis was to call a family meeting. This first meeting set the tone for the next four months. After agreeing on a day and time, this is pretty much how they all went:

- Gather together at Peter's in person or by phone
- Go around the circle with updates
- Discuss options
- Make jokes. Yes, cry too, but jokes were essential.
- Report on progress
- Make more jokes.
- Assign tasks
- Believe healing is possible
- Set a date for the next meeting

These meetings had a regular cast of characters: Peter and Elyn, of course and usually Zena and Morgan, their 22 and 27 year old kids. Darshan, my older brother, came from Virginia every 2 or 3 weeks and called in when he was not in town. Lee and I were regulars, trying to at least stop in every day. Our oldest son, Moses who lived 45 minutes away, attended almost every meeting and often his 18 year old son Jyasi came too. Shanti and Avi, both in NYC, came often and Kiara was there for every meeting (physically or virtually) even though she lived in LA. My niece and nephew in Santa Fe shared research or suggestions often.

Eventually we settled on a two-pronged treatment protocol for Peter. One involved supplements and diet and the other focused on high doses of cannabis oil with supplies shipped to us from Colorado. We attempted to make both of these protocols as streamlined and achievable as possible since the majority of the daily burden fell on Elyn.

During this time, despite difficulty breathing and overwhelming fatigue, Peter was still very much the brother I have always relied on. The jokes and sardonic commentary still flowed. When either Zena or Morgan was there, he sparkled. He maintained his interest in the world, but I could soon feel a distance, like he was trying, for us, but the world was already beckoning him in a different direction.

Closely following New Year's, barely four months after hearing the devastating diagnosis, Peter took his final breath in his bed with his wife Elyn lying next to him. Three days before this he had convened the final family meeting. There he rallied enough to ask his family for permission to go. It was too hard, the suffering was overwhelming, he was so tired, he needed to let go. Despite being in a lot of pain and almost unable to sit up, he still managed to make a couple of Peter jokes and we caught a glimmer of those twinkling Peter eyes. We cried, his son Morgan and daughter Zena both bid for a little more time, offering to rub his back round the clock, but Peter somehow knew that time had run out for him. Finally the meeting came to a close, Darshan and Kiara hung up, and we dispersed.

Hospice was called in for a morphine drip. Three days later, even they were surprised when it was all over. My wonderful brother had passed on and so many of us were left behind to try and imagine a life without him.

At his large memorial almost everyone wanted to tell a Peter story. There was more laughter than tears. Both Zena and Morgan offered wonderful speeches overflowing with hilarious lists of things they had learned from their father. People shared stories of his sweet jokes, his tennis and basketball games, his laughter and many work stories.

Sarah said, "I will say 3 words about Peter: warmth, humor, kindness and always support and encouragement."

Mark said "In my first training with him, I thought of him as a God. Any chance to work with him, I took it. He stands forever as my model: if I am doing it at all like Peter Glassman, I am doing it right."

Another colleague said, "Some people use humor as power, others to hurt or brag, but Peter used humor to serve, to wake up the room, to throw his co-trainer a life line, to build connections."

The stories about work and play, laughter and generosity poured out and followed us all home to begin our new lives without Peter. Not an easy task. But every birthday Niko will hear about the legacy for justice and freedom that he has inherited from his Great Uncle Peter.

Chocolate Chip Cookie Recipe

It is time for your celebration: birthday, anniversary, or any time you want to celebrate. Please pass the cake. But wait! How about a plate of cookies instead? Cakes can fall, they can mess up, and they are often too sweet or too dry. But you can never go wrong with a good batch of chocolate chip cookies, and they will make almost everyone happy.

Okay. Now we must get into the realm of the sacred. My family has travelled far and wide searching for great chocolate chip cookies. Some people look for pristine beaches, others for wild animal sightings. I know families who search for their ancestors and others who trace historical battle sights. We, on the other hand, go on chocolate chip cookie quests. There have been numerous disappointments: dry, crumbly, too few chips, too many chips, the wrong chips, too sweet, not sweet enough. For the sake of research, we have suffered through many inferior creations that should not have the right to be called chocolate chip cookies.

But we have also come across a few truly transcendent creations. There was that one somewhere in Hulu on the Big Island of Hawaii. We were visiting Shanti who was working there. Sitting on a lanai beneath a huge tree swaying under the weight of ripening avocados, we enjoyed an almost perfect cookie. In Iceland, it came with multi-grains and seeds surrounding the chips. It didn't make Lee's top ten list, but I thought it had some merit. And, of course, there is Levain's in Harlem, conveniently located around the corner from Shanti's apartment. That amazing cookie must weigh half a pound, is formed by an ice cream scoop and could be called a meal all by itself.

We are almost ready to propose a labeling system complete with ratings. It would make it so much easier for people to arrive in a new town and know just where to go for a four-star crispy cookie in Baltimore or the highly-rated chewy one in Chicago. Devotees could post their winning selections, and a carefully elected panel would judge them and announce the findings annually.

Despite all the cookies we have tried and loved, I am proud to inform you that there may be no better chocolate chip cookie than the one that comes out of our oven on a regular basis. This has become Lee's specialty, and all regular visitors know that the chances are pretty good they will find hot cookies on the table sometime after dinner.

Cookie baking is a highly evolved art form and must be taken seriously. A perfect cookie is neither a joke nor an accident. Rather, it involves an expertise that is the result of effort, foresight, and talent in equal measure. So come on by for a taste, but remember to have proper respect for the sacred cookie.

Lee has given me his generous permission to share his, up until now, top-secret instructions on making a stupendous batch of chocolate cookies. First you must be sworn in to the Society of CCCC (Chocolate Chip Cookie Connoisseurs). Here we go!

Ingredients

- 2 1/4 cups all-purpose flour (you will probably use less)
- 1 teaspoon baking soda
- 1 cup (2 sticks) butter, softened
- 3/4 cup granulated sugar
- 3/4 cup packed brown sugar
- 2 large eggs
- 1 teaspoon water
- 2 teaspoon vanilla
- Semi-Sweet Chocolate Chips
- 1 cup chopped nuts

Remember the recipe on the back of the Tollhouse cookie package? Who doesn't? That is a good starting place. But (said in a booming Obi wan Kenobi voice) "that is only the beginning."

1. Take the two sticks of butter.
2. Stop right there. You are now at a crucial step in the process. The butter must be soft, but not completely melted. In our house, where there is no microwave, and it is rather chilly most of the year, we warm the butter by placing it in a metal bowl that sits in some hot water inside our cast iron pan. When it is soft, but not all melted, the butter must then be beaten well. And I mean really well beaten. Don't skimp on this step. It should turn a smooth shade of golden sunlight. Then and only then do you:

3. Add the sugar and brown sugar and beat some more.

4. Mix the eggs into the bowl.

Here we come to a major fork in the road: flavoring. The recipe on the Tollhouse bag calls for 1 teaspoon of vanilla.

5. Use real vanilla. My niece, Nirinjan, an outstanding cook, makes her own. Double the vanilla. Or make it half vanilla and half almond extract. Take a deep breath. Mmmm. There are healing qualities in that vanilla smell. You know, they say houses sell more quickly with the smell of cookies baking or simply the vanilla smell dispersed.

6. Consider the add-ons. This is what separates the good cookies from the great ones! Personal preference and a little bit of playfulness can enter here. It is not a time to become frivolous or glib. We take our cookies VERY seriously, but you have some choices when it comes to add-ons. Grated orange peel is very good, as is cinnamon. Caramel slivers are a possibility or a little coarse salt crystals can be dispersed. And, of course, almond extract can be added, but be careful, don't get carried away.

Are you ready to beat in the dry ingredients?

7. Combine: 1 teaspoon salt and 1 teaspoon baking powder (or even a little less) and the flour. Be careful with the flour. Less is more here. Many people make the mistake of making cookies that are dry and pasty. This

is likely to be caused by too much flour. Do not use the entire 2 and 1/4 cups. Add a cup and 3/4 and then the chips and wait.

8. Add the chocolate chips! (trumpet plays loudly here!!) This, too, it is a matter of taste. Though I am a connoisseur of dark chocolate, two cups of chips are too many as far as I am concerned. And since we are on chocolate, here is where the rubber hits the road. You can use the recipe on the back of the Tollhouse chips, but you must use the chips in the Ghirardelli dark package, not the gold one. Or if you are feeling adventurous, use a bar of good dark chocolate, at least 65% chocolate. Place it on a cutting board, take a good knife, and chop your own chips. These can be chunks or slivers.

9. Wow! All you have left is the nuts. I love nuts in my cookies, but you can leave them out even though I do not recommend it. We use walnuts, but pecans are also great. Chop them, not too finely, and throw them in.

At this point, you should have all your ingredients in the bowl except for a small reserve of flour. This is where Lee does a test batch of two cookies. In this way, he can determine if it needs more flour. Impatient as always, I usually skip this step, but perfection is not my strong point. Some people recommend placing the batter in the refrigerator for a couple of hours, allowing the dry ingredients to absorb the wet ingredients, but that is not happening in this household.

10. Place the tray in a 350 degree oven for about ten minutes. Keep an eye on them. Do not overcook

because they will continue to cook for a little while after they are removed. Take them out of the oven. Carefully slide them onto a rack. Now try to wait a few minutes so that you do not burn your tongue and ENJOY! You may soon be voting for your own cookies as the best in the world.

Top: Grown children
Bottom: The Barbershop Boys 2015

Clockwise Top Left: Moses and Niko. A young Peter. Tessa, Jyasi and Zena. Shanti on a rooftop garden;

Top: Climate march 2015.
Bottom: French Canals 2012.

Top: Front Porch 2015.
Bottom: Little Tokyo, Los Angeles, CA.

Acknowledgement

How do you thank a lifetime of love, support, and kindness? Shout it from the rooftop! Thank you to my family – I hit the jackpot this time. What an adventure it has been. I am so thankful. A special pirouette to my one and only, what a ride we have been on! I owe you the sun, and the moon, and the stars. Stick around for repayment. I am in awe of you who are the best of me and so much more—Moses, Kiara, Shanti, and Avi. You are my motivation, my teachers, my heart. Your lives have become inspirations to me. An extra shout out to Shanti who, as usual, brought beauty and and to Kiara who efficiently, but gently, came in and closed the deal.

I am an avid student of my now bigger-than-me grandchildren Jyasi and Tessa: you keep me off balance and make me want to leave the world a little better than I found it. A bundle of thanks to Temo and Dylan and of course sweet, loving Niko, for coming into my life, teaching me some new tricks and expanding my heart. To Joanna and Rosaly who offer thoughtful inspiration.

I am so lucky to have a wise, elder brother who guards the memories, shares the soundtrack and offers comfort. And of course Peter, who never stopped encouraging me in whatever latest scheme I shared with him as he encircled me with the best love and

300

laughter a sister could have. My intrepid Aunt Irene, a treasure trove of ideas for a more just planet. To my father, are you reading this now, Dad? And to Mom,too. To my professors Reverend/Dr, Judy Campbell and Dr. Debbie Sherman who whipped me into a better thinker. Kathryn Tracy keeps showing up for me and Tanya LaPlante and Jocelyn Arem continued to tell me I could do it. Lin Murphy, my soul sister, read many of these essays and offered precious friendship and long walks and Bev allowed a little of her can-do attitude to rub off on me. And of course hallelujahs to my almost actual sister, Jody Nagel, who protected me, prodded me, and gave me the best writing retreat a gal could ever hope to find. I am grateful for my time on this planet. I am truly grateful!

> *Do not be daunted by the enormity of the world's grief.*
> *Do justly, now.*
> *Love mercy, now.*
> *Walk humbly, now.*
> *You are not obligated to complete the work,*
> *but neither are you free to abandon it.*

The Talmud